Editorial

Why was I so affected (see News and Notes below) by the story of the beetle infestation of the millennium-old Hungarian Pannonhalma Archabbey? It has something to do with the way in which the sudden disturbance in the permanency of a library affects the stability of the librarian and the readers themselves.

When at the start of this century I moved apartments in Manchester, the men from Pickford's sized up my meagre furnishings and gave me an estimate. It was so reasonable that I drew to their attention the book-lined walls.

'All that's to come with us.'

'That's fine,' they said. 'We've taken it into account.'

In the end there were fifty-seven cases of books to be moved two streets, from a fourth-floor flat in Granby Row to a fourth-floor flat on Sackville Street. The movers had not factored in how much books weigh, how much space the flat little rectangles multiplied a few thousand times fill. To make matters worse, early in the move the Sackville Street lift failed. Moving furniture was a doddle but the books were worse than any albatross.

When Walter Benjamin moved house in 1931, he wrote his essay 'Unpacking My Library: A Speech on Collecting'. Alberto Manguel recalls,

> he used the occasion of pulling his almost two thousand books out of their boxes to muse on the privileges and responsibilities of a reader. Benjamin was moving from the house he had shared with his wife until their acrimonious divorce the previous year to a small furnished apartment in which he would live alone, he said, for the first time in his life, 'like an adult'. Benjamin was then 'at the threshold of forty and without property, position, home or assets'. It might not be entirely mistaken to see his meditation on books as a counterpoise to the breakup of his marriage.

Manguel himself wrote a compelling book entitled *Packing My Library,* published by Yale in 2018. Having lived for a decade and a half in a medieval stone presbytery in the South of France with his partner, and a library of 35,000 books housed in a converted barn, he was obliged to move. Packing his books was a creative trauma for 'the world's foremost melancholic bibliophile'. His library was a kind of autobiography and its packing away 'something of a self-obituary'.

After twenty-five years in our Victorian offices, Carcanet Press and *PN Review* were bombed out of the first home in the Corn Exchange, Manchester (1996). After a few years' looking for a new home with our dusty, damaged books in rescue boxes, we washed up in Cross Street. Twenty-seven years on, we were driven to relocate – for ever, it is to be hoped – to our present location in Manchester University Library. The removal agents this time were experienced book movers and the transition was meticulously organised. They tucked the spine-out books and the material that had been tucked behind them (duplicates, forgotten titles, Christmas cards, bus tickets) among the 'public' books, waking up a vast fossil-life.

The one unexpected circumstance of the move was that the shelving in the renovated offices had not been completed. For almost a year after the move, our books were stored on dozens of two-sided library trolleys. Our collection within the University library was in creative disorder for months, neither chaos (because some of the books retained an alphabetical sequence), nor cosmos (because there was no predictable sequence to the trolleys). We were continually confronted with titles produced half a century ago, mingling with new books, and with the fossil material which recalled departed colleagues, authors and forgotten species. Even a few shards of glass from the bombed-out Corn Exchange.

We were driven back on our electronic resources, the files of PDFs of our titles becoming our major textual resource. The books grew less relevant as time passed: the apotheosis of remote working, estranged and even alienated from the very products we were selling into the world. The trolleyed library weighs tonnes, but it could be virtually stored and shared on laptops where dust did not gather or thieves break in and steal.

PN Review's physical world has now righted itself. New shelves again groan under weight of paper. Things hide behind the magazines and books and arrange for our heirs their eventual surprises. A new form of memory is being generated, an alphabetised chronology drawing on at least three long-term stable periods, each disrupted by events beyond our control. Every change ends in discovery and rediscovery. History is differently inflected. Yards of books by MacDiarmid, Ashbery, Morgan, Jennings, Sisson, Davie, Ford, Graves, Laura Riding extend, but they look different now, spaced out, becoming antique. *PN Review* manifests in all its phases, from the six demi-octavo hardback 'magazines' with which we began to the quarterly and six-times-yearly A4 paperbacks. 290 items, almost a complete set. Or if we count this issue, 291... The question is, how hungry are the beetles in Pannonhalma Archabbey, and are they travelling north?

Letters to the Editor

Birdsong

Apropos Lesley Harrison's 'Do Birds Sing?' (*PNR* 284), the poet Douglas Oliver, in his novel *The Harmless Building*, has the seagulls overhead screaming 'Jacques Lacan! Jacques Lacan!' I mentioned this to a poetry researcher who was living in Brighton who retorted that the seagulls above her house were screaming 'Melanie Klein! Melanie Klein!'

Anthony Barnett

*

A Silly Voice

Dear Sir, I drink whisky every day; I eat grouse and wild salmon; I've a Harris tweed coat; I admire the martial tone of the pipes and drums, *nemo me impune lacessit* and all that.

I've gorged on Tartan Noir *romans policiers*. Old William Wallace Robson supervised my Master's thesis. W.S. Graham is a poet I especially like. But... Unlike the writer of *PNR* 283's editorial column, Graham did not feel the need to put on a silly voice. All this 'Scots' cobblers? It is just English in a stage accent.

Nanetheless.

Come off it!

And *accoontit...*

In ither wards...

Scots winna thole deconstruction...

Do me a favour!

The idea that speaking English like Rob Roy as well as in a more normal way makes you bilingual is just a bogus excuse for jocks not to *learn* another language to achieve bilingual status.

I park it in the same bucket as many other forms of nonsense to which we are all bid bow down.

To be discussed.

Yours faithfully,
Christopher Garnett

Zounds! If I wer Christopher Garnett, I widnae wad tae mak 'mortal foes' o' sik a poke o' 'open pussies'. He may wak wan mornin' wi' Gerard Carruthers sittin' awn his chest singin' the 'Jeely Piece Song'!

Yowres trewly,
Sir Hairy Larder

News and Notes

Queen Sofia again! • On 7 May 2025, Luis Alberto de Cuenca was announced as recipient of this year's Queen Sofia Award for Iberoamerican Poetry. It was the 34th year of the award, which carries a €42,100 purse and is given to mark the collected works of a living author. The poet is said to have a 'clear, precise style', his gaze trained 'critically on the literary tradition with a tone that can be characterised as ironic or melancholy', according to the director of National Patrimony, María Dolores Menéndez. He is 'a bridge-builder' between ancient mythology and the modern world.

One element in the prize is publication: his work will be issued in an annotated edition by a distinguished professor of literature at the University of Salamanca: the kiss of immortality and the kiss of poetic death attuned. Such plaudits render the poet virtually marmoreal. Queen Sofia herself will present the award to the still breathing poet later in the year. When he received the news, he was especially delighted that he would receive the award at the Queen's hand. He currently serves on the board of the National Library of Spain and of the Prado Museum and is a previous selector for the Queen Sofia Award. He has written over thirty books of poems, twenty of essays, two novels and 'countless translations'. From 1996 to 2000 he was the director of the National Library, and Secretary of State of Culture for Spain until 2004.

Derry O'Sullivan • It was reported that the Irish-language poet Derry O'Sullivan has died in Paris. He was eighty-one. Born in west Cork, he studied Latin, Greek and Philosophy at University College Cork, became a Capuchin monk, was ordained a priest in 1969 and sent to Paris. In 1970 he resigned the priesthood, surviving as a teacher of English at the Sorbonne, the Institut Catholique de Paris and the Institut Supérieur d'Electronique de Paris. His three poetry collections in Irish were *Cá bhfuil do Iúdás?* (1987), *Cá bhfuil Tiarna Talún l'Univers?* (1994), and *An bhfuil cead agam dul amach, más é do thoil é?* (2009), as well as *An Lá go dTáinig Siad* (2005), an extended work about the Nazi takeover of Paris in 1940. His poetry was translated into French. A pamphlet of his poems translated into English appeared in 1987, and a version of his poem 'Marbhghin 1943' by Kaarina Hollo won the Stephen Spender Prize for poetry in translation in 2012.

Out of Africa • *Poetry* magazine announced the selection of Nigerian poet Maryhilda Obasiota Ibe as a 2025 Ruth Lilly and Dorothy Sargent Rosenberg Poetry Fellow. Jerry Chiemeke reported that the fellowship was awarded in recognition of the poet's contributions to Poetry (with a capital P), and is worth $27,000, to be applied 'as she sees fit in the development of her craft'. She is one of five poets to receive the annual fellowships. The others include Jada Renée Allen, DeeSoul Carson, Andres Cordoba and Aris Kian.

Common Sense • In a rare victory for common sense, *Publishers' Weekly* reported on 18 August that a Florida court upheld the freedom to read in 'PRH v. Gibson'. Nathalie op de Beeck wrote: 'In an order that sets a strong precedent for keeping books on public school library shelves, the U.S. District Court for the Middle District of Florida has upheld the freedom to read in Penguin Random House v. Gibson. Filed in August 2024' – the case taking a full year to reach a conclusion – 'the lawsuit challenges key provisions of Florida House Bill 1069, which was signed into law by Florida Governor Ron DeSantis in May 2023 and purports to bar "pornographic" materials and content that "depicts or describes sexual content" from school and classroom libraries.' Florida had facilitated it so that parents could object to public school contents. 'The challenged materials are then removed from K–12 student access, ostensibly for review and often on the basis of words and sentences taken out of context.' The Court declared, 'It is readily apparent to the Court that the statute fails strict scrutiny. The state's prohibition of material that "describes sexual conduct" is overbroad and unconstitutional.' Dan Novack, Vice President and associate general counsel at PRH, in a statement made on behalf of the plaintiff group, said: 'The Court also struck down the State's vague "I know it when I see it" standard, reinforcing the essential role of librarians and educators in selecting books for students' independent reading.' Other plaintiffs in the case include the other four Big Five publishers, Sourcebooks, the Authors Guild, five authors, and two parents of Florida students who found that Jack Kerouac's *On the Road* and Toni Morrison's *The Bluest Eye* had been pulled from shelves at their public high schools. Judge Mendoza put his decision in the context of other significant rulings around the freedom to read, among them PRH v. Robbins – a current lawsuit challenging Iowa Senate Bill 496 and the removal of hundreds of books from public schools – and the nearly twenty-year-old decision in ACLU v. Miami-Dade County, concerning Miami public schools' censorship of a children's series that included a travel book titled *Vamos a Cuba* (A Visit to Cuba).

The underground avant-garde • In November, World Poetry will release new translations from Arabic and Greek. Samer Abu Hawwash's *Ruins and Other Poems* 'stand upon ancient and modern ruins, engaging with the archetypal Arabic qasida and its echoes in the present, set against a backdrop of exile, displacement, and genocide. Abu Hawwash rearranges the elements of poetry in the Arabic tradition – the site of the ruin, the journey, and the return home – in search of closure or consolation.' The poems are translated from Arabic by Huda J. Fakhreddine. Also projected is Phoebe Giannisi's *Homerica*. She is described as 'one of Greece's foremost poetic voices', and the book will appear in 'a revised second edition, offering a contemporary Odyssey of loss, longing, motherhood, and metamorphosis'. Karen Van Dyck calls her verse 'a wonderful combination of the classical and the underground avant-garde'. Ann Carson says this is 'an unusually excellent translation' by Brian Sneeden, with a preface by Eleni Sikelianos.

Happy Birthday! • It is twenty years since the Poetry Archive, that enormous resource of recorded poetry (in the poet's own voice) and a key legacy of Andrew Motion's Poet Laureateship, went online. One of its most impressive recent developments has been 'The Poetry of South Asia', described as a 'living and evolving digital and audio-visual collection [which] explores the breadth, influence and poetic lineage of South Asia'.

Beetle Mania • The millennium-old Pannonhalma Archabbey, founded in 996, a UNESCO World Heritage site, is a Benedictine monastery that contains Hungary's oldest library. It is among Hungary's oldest cultural assets. At present a quarter of its 400,000 book collection is threatened by a plague of drugstore or bread beetles that could prove fatal to it. Restorers are trying to remove the affected books from their primeval shelves, crating them up and disinfecting them. The beetles like dried foods including flour, grains and spices. They also like the adhesives used in binding books, and antique adhesives are especially tasty to them. 'This is an advanced insect infestation which has been detected in several parts of the library, so the entire collection is classified as infected and must be treated all at the same time', said Zsófia Edit Hajdu, chief restorer on the project. The intensity of the infestation is unprecedented. The beetles revealed their presence in the proliferation of dust they created. Then the holes in the spines were discovered. The abbey, four years older than the Hungarian Empire, survived the Ottoman invasion and all the other historical incursions. The beetles might prove its nemesis though no expense is being spared in defeating them. The crated books are put in hermetically sealed plastic sacks. Oxygen is removed and after a few weeks it is hoped that the foes will have suffocated. Then the books will be hoovered clean and reshelved or restored. Even though the potential disaster is happening in Hungary, it's suggested that the culprit behind the beetles is *climate change*.

FROM THE ARCHIVE

from **PNR 185, vol. 35, no. 3**
January – February 2009

Contributors to the issue included Carola Luther, Adam Thorpe, Chris McCully and Stephanie Burt

Prizes

Elaine Feinstein

A cold wind. A clear sky. Wet branches
sizzle this morning in the sunlight.
Take no notice of the man behind the curtain.
You can always get back to Kansas. If you know
where home is, you don't have a problem.
Consider this lonely man, unshaven, smiling.

[...]

On Balance: Part One

ANTHONY VAHNI CAPILDEO

It was a good night to see the Perseids. We headed out past the lighthouse and sat on the slope of the old deep-water harbour. The sky separated into clouds and moonlight, like curds and whey in a blue-black cup. Haar rose like an army of mist from the sea. An aeroplane silently burnt along. So many trails of light; we always knew what we were looking for, seldom what we were looking at... Radiant can be a noun, when you speak of meteor showers. The meteors' apparent point of departure, to earth-bound observers like us, is called their 'radiant'. We spotted sporadics, heading at varying speeds and on different trajectories – that one to Edinburgh, we said; that one to Fife. To the southwest of Scotland's capital, someone let off almost unnoticeable fireworks, as if without a murmur. Festivals were happening. We looked at the stars and talked about balance.

Perseids have their radiant in the constellation Perseus, named for the ancient Greek hero famous for decapitating the beautiful, paralysing Medusa of the snaky locks. 'Look nah', his statues boast on repeat in the civilized world, as he displays her head in one hand, held casually at his side, like a shopping bag; the mirror-like shield in the other hand, winged sandals on his feet. It is a classic moment of fixity; or is it? Do we not imagine her open eyes when they were in process of opening, the focus of her blank glare shifting, the creatures composing her hair lifting to scent the breeze, and her head swaying with the pulse of the great killer's grasp? It is a questionable morality and an impossible aesthetic that would have us agree to become the statue's statues, fixing the shower of our mind's light on *this moment, now, here*. A warrior holding up a detached body part invites us to a story with a before and an after. We might find ourselves in it. Such once-for-all stories are too satisfying not to be engineered to recur.

Balance is one of those words where French nudges out English, for me. This means that *balance* itself shifts its weight; sometimes the first syllable is heavy, sometimes the second syllable is heavier but the final consonant nasalizes and skims off, hinting at another opening out, the syllable's finitude reverting to breath's unfinishing. This childhood word of changing stress, balance, *balance*. Is it the kitchen scales, or the Dégas ballerinas paused in flight on the decorated mirror used to check your plaited hair? Balance, a pendulum word, going to and fro. Later, when I tried to nudge out French with Italian, I turned to the familiar stories of western classical myth; the home comfort of tradition – but Roberto Calasso's *Le nozze di Cadmo e Armonia* (1988) placed a sacrificed girl swaying before his reader's mind. My memory of that book falsifies it so that this scene is front and centre, no matter the story, multiplying pine groves and other locations where the body of a girl swings as if it is inevitable that we mark time this way; sad, but rather beautiful – a balance.

The annoying film *Wings of Desire* (1987), so close in time to Calasso's tome, suspends a conventionally sexually desirable cis-female trapeze artist in the middle of the screen, coercing us to share the gradually fixated gaze of a human-presenting masculine-appearing angel. As with my memory of Calasso, I over-remember this scene's recurrence, and how she is vertical, while he bunches up. Memory is unfair to balance. Was she swaying, slightly? Did the camera-god allow her gravity as well as grace? As with stage corpses, did we see her breathing? What bothered me about her? Perhaps the balance, the either/or offered to the viewer – for I was not sophisticated enough to distance myself from identifying with the lit-up characters on offer; to sit, as it were, on the rocks and scrutinize the skies for scientifically-announced, secretly waywardly delightful signs. Far too invested in the absolute weirdness of angels' unimaginability, their churring multiplicity and inside-outside eyes, I neither wanted to identify the angel as angel, nor wanted, since I myself identified as girl, that hanging body to serve as the exemplary embodiment of the aspirational feminine.

We do not like words like 'trigger' – we would have to deploy the giggle of dismissal – but this acrobat triggered the memory of sway, what it had been like to become girl. The way she hangs there makes me remember visiting seamstresses in Trinidad. It was normal to have clothes made – imports were expensive, in those days – and to enter the seamstress's porch, where an elderly relative was settled doll-like in a rocking chair, unspeaking but with a cloudless smile in her blue eyes. This text, these woven words, recall the fabric of those indoor lives, the doilies, the net curtains, the silk flowers. The clients' textiles, bales of cloth propped up under and in between dark wood, cut-out and basted 'pieces' of garments, schoolday gingham, churchgoer charmeuse satin, half-made for trying on, pinned together, hanging at many heights.

The bead curtain to the house's back parts, a hard boundary for clients. See-through. Hand-strung. Dust falling from the brightness in the air, and pieces to be fitted to body parts, and in the north-east trade winds, everything, a little, swaying. Raise your arms and be still to be measured, to have cloth pinned up around you. The mirror to check the fall, the line. Clean hands of the seamstress, her bad haircut and cheap shorts, bright eyes. Verbally beaten and begged for impossible deadlines for occasion dresses. Her ability to make a costume from looking at a magazine photo, her overwork, her sewing outfits for herself in synthetic fabrics, the resinous furniture, her sweating. The shower of light of the bead curtain drew my attention as I made every effort to stay motionless. The curtain was privacy. It was theatre. It becomes a memory motif, that dressmaking scene, and how a life's work made people into girls and women.

Antigone was one of the imaginary girls whose family was as intimate to my childhood as the pieces for trying on. In the Nazi-occupied Paris of the 1940s, the French playwright Jean Anouilh staged a work based on Sophocles' drama of authority, challenge, duty and freedom. Antigone defies the King by attempting to bury her rebellious brother, whose corpse has been left exposed to rot as a reminder not to rise up against the King – the same King whose son, not incidentally, is her beloved fiancé. (Don't make it political, Antigone.) My mother brought back from the Paris of the 1950s and 1960s a kind of new folklore, about the stupid soldiers who so worshipped the western classical world to which they laid claim as their exclusive heritage that they sat in the theatre dutifully to see the Greek play and applauded, never realizing that the wicked authorities represented them, and Antigone, the truth-telling heroine, encouraged French resistance. Everyone held their breath, expecting the soldiers to jump up and arrest them; but the soldiers were too stupid. I heard about this when I was little, at bedtime and mealtimes.

So many questions only occurred to me this summer, the summer of the Perseids, as I sat in Edinburgh's Institut Français, waiting for the curtains to part and the action of Mythography theatre's English-language production of Anouilh's *Antigone* to begin. The stage set consisted of one chair and these curtains, large, heavy and translucent. Through them, the audience could glimpse the few actors needed to set an ambiguous tragedy going. In front of them, the Chorus, leather-jacketed, cigarette a burning point of light, making eye contact, pacing.

I had given the literary festivals a miss. There is one long-running war, which seems to inspire programmers to a self-imposed system of internal weights and measures – one must programme writers from 'both sides' onto the same panels, or at least have them circulating in the same space, to achieve 'balance'. Forced trauma-teaming, would you say, or creative intimacy? Yet all other wars are exempt from juxtaposing their speaking candidates in such ways... Anyway, I went to this Fringe show instead, preferring the embodied word, revisiting the dead and imaginary friends of my youth. As we waited, I felt Edinburgh timeslip to Paris. What if some of the soldiers secretly did not want to be Nazis? What if some of the actors were Nazi sympathizers? What if members of the Résistance were in the audience? What if some of the actors were freedom fighters? What were the threads between the human beings the darkly lit theatre contained?

You cannot think like that. That was then. This is now. Think of Antigone wanting to bury her brother, a simple gesture of respect. An extreme state makes it extreme. But I think of the parents scraping human tissue hanging like bead curtains from what were interiors and mourning it as their children. Now. There.

On John Boydell's engraving of *A View taken near Limehouse Bridge, looking down the Thames* (1751)

FAWZIA MURADALI KANE

We know this view. It is familiar, and its unchanging parts have become anchors for our mind's home. The river flows. The sky stretches over. The shingle and sand scrape along the foreshore. These have been so before us, over the centuries – millennia even – and will persist beyond our days.

How many times have we seen such skies over us in this place? The light wind prevails from the southwest (clue: the ship's pennants), across the river's curve from Pageant Stairs, billowing and sweeping the clouds over the north bank's rooftops. From the shadows and lightness of the sky above the larger ship to the right, we notice the sun is shining from the southeast. The angles of drawn rays and cast shadows tell us it is around mid-morning. Light clothing on the people, smokeless chimneys and washing put out to dry on the terraces points to a summer's day. Smoke swirls upwards from a couple of doors up from where The Grapes pub is now. The kitchen's fire has been lit. The cook of the house is hard at work.

Aquatint versions exist of this engraving, but the skies in those depictions are pastel coloured, prettiness spread over the quaintness of the washed walls below. This colouring in must have been some years later. Memory changes perception, although it's likely the colourists were others who were not present when this particular scene was sketched.

Perhaps there is such accuracy in this work because John Boydell was the son of a surveyor. The view is 'taken near Limehouse Bridge', which is now the modern Swing Bridge next to Victoria Wharf. Blyth's Wharf's pier did not exist in 1751, so this view is from the river itself, eye level with the rear terraces of Narrow Street. Boydell could only have been looking from a vessel moored on the river itself. The tide is low. A few lighter craft rest on

the foreshore. A Thames barge leans against the old brick river wall, where Blyth's Wharf's pier would be built in 1923. We are holding a snapshot of the working lives, and the life itself, of our river on this clement summer's morning of 1751.

Boydell dots the shingle and damp sand as striations that follow the wash of the river's edge. There are more boats moored on the river. Tristan Gooley in his book *How to Read Water* tells of detecting tidal currents by looking at boats at anchor, how they can be seen 'pointing dependably into the current like a weathercock'. George Stillwell, my late mariner colleague, called the tide at its highest or lowest 'slack' water. The current is at a standstill then, he told us, then it rises or lowers. Accelerating to its halfway point, the current then slows down to slackness. This is the safest period for our marine contractor workmates to enter the water and secure foundations into the riverbed.

Over the years, I have watched out for this tidal point from the houses' terraces. When I watch the river's surface from here, I imagine it moves as a slow breath, almost imperceptible, pulling itself off the foreshore in its inhalation towards its pause: slack water. The hours will pass while the river's water-breath returns. It will rise as the full exhale of the swell until it washes against the shoulders of Another Time.

But there is no such slackening in Boydell's view. The passenger boats are full, heading downriver, taking advantage of the current as the river ebbs. In the foreground, two lightermen stand in their craft, pushing *against* the current away from the larger ship. In 1751, the Pool of London did not have enough off-load docks built yet. Ships would have to moor in the river for their cargo to be moved onto smaller boats, to be taken to the main wharfs. What is the cargo on this ship? Spices and tea from India or China? Sugar and rum from enslaved plantations in the West Indies? Did the wind carry these scents towards the houses along Narrow Street?

Now let us examine these houses of 1751. The drawing shows a heavy brick retaining wall that enclosed the cellars and earthen foundations of the houses along this part of Narrow Street. We know this still exists – although what we see here is embedded in additional layers built over to strengthen and protect, across the centuries. We know that waste riddlings of nearby sixteenth-century lime burners are buried under these houses, leaving a thick layer of lime. We discovered this strange white layer during our twenty-first-century basement excavations.

There are ladders from the foreshore leading up to the back of the ground floors. Along the front would have been shops facing the street, serving the river industries: chandlers, sail makers, rope makers and other boating suppliers. Above (what is now) nos. 90 and 92 Narrow Street – then called Fore Street – is a large sign boasting 'WINE'. The census some years later stated a 'victualler' lived there. What a vital service for tired river people! The shape of no. 92's roof is still the same to this day.

On the drawing, we can see little outcrops, overhanging the river wall: latrines for s(h)itting on, or emptying kitchen rubbish or bedroom chamber pots into the river. As in our modern times, the rear terraces run along the roofs of the ground floor extensions. Nos. 88 to 78 Narrow Street are clearly shown as a coherent block of terraced houses. No. 76, the current site of The Grapes, is drawn as a neat flat-fronted elevation, slightly stepped back from its neighbours. We can find this wall now on its upper floors, still stepped back from no. 78's rear elevation. But the 1751 building is also wider. So some time later, between then and Dickens's first visit, the building was halved, with the Harbour Master's office and lodgings inserted next door. It appears that over the years, the accretion of rooms – was this always an inn? – caused the remnants of this earlier eighteenth-century building to become embedded in the 'newer' parts, until it has become the pub we know today. And westwards from The Grapes's earlier ghosts to the modern Papermill Wharf, the rest is also gone – replaced by warehouses and twentieth-century developers' cupidity.

But the river and its skies will remain. Even though modernity's engines have conquered the currents, and their frothy wakes race past us, river vessels must still follow the ebb and flow. The foreshore will be shaped by its shingle and scraped by mudlarks. The tides keep their rhythm of rise and fall, spring and neap. The waxing and waning of the moon, even the equinoctial sun, will always play their part on the water, well beyond the vagaries of our human lives.

Letter from Brunnenburg

STEPHEN ROMER

From 8–11 July, the 31st bi-annual Ezra Pound International Conference (EPIC) was held at Brunnenburg Castle in the Italian Tyrol, home of the poet's daughter Mary de Rachewiltz. Over one hundred scholars and poets, from five continents, many accompanied by family, converged at what proved in many ways to be a conference for the ages, and a *nostos* of sorts: since it was to Brunnenburg that Pound came to rest, on 12 July 1958, after his arrival back in Italy following his twelve-year internment in Washington DC at Saint Elizabeth's. This mood was fostered by the conference theme, 'Light and Memory in Ezra Pound', and the fact that Mary's 100th birthday fell on 9 July. Our celebration of her and her exemplary custodianship of one of the most contested literary legacies of the Modernist era was at the heart of the conference. Mary de Rachewiltz, Pound's 'carissima bambina', early on undertook the translation into Italian of the *Cantos*, and her father was giving her advice and instructions even from the internment camp in Pisa. But we were also celebrating the recent publication of her own Italian poems, gathered by Massimo Bacigalupo of Rapallo, undisputed *capo* of Pound studies in Italy. Mary did not herself read, but responded to the readings and remarks of others, by her son Siegfried de Rachewiltz, and the two mainstays of EPIC, Walter Baumann, the doyen of Pound studies, and long-serving secretary John Gery.

Brunnenburg Castle, almost preposterously romantic where it nestles in a dip on a steep hillside, surrounded by the Dolomites, is a kind of vortex. The two main conference rooms are just off the central spiral staircase, and on the rough plaster, in an unbroken upward chain, hang artworks, most notably Dorothy Pound's striking black-and-white 'vorticist' designs for the cover of *Ripostes*. The seminar rooms themselves contain behind glass the poet's typewriter, and many of the notebook jottings that came to form the final section of the *Cantos* as we have them now, the *Drafts & Fragments*. Dominating a shaded parterre within the precincts of the cobbled courtyard is a bronze cast of Henri Gaudier-Brzeska's giant 'Hieratic Head' of the poet, which was carved in London when Pound befriended the sculptor and paid for a block of marble. Seen from behind, the head is entirely phallic, a brazen cock crow of 'direct carving'. Great golden cockerels do in fact strut about the courtyard and on the 'Hilaritas' terrace, crowing competitively at chosen moments.

Regarding 'Pound studies', the EPIC conference is a reliable indicator of new directions. With fourteen papers devoted entirely to Pound and China (and the East more generally), more analysis of his China Cantos is being done by a new generation of Poundians that include young Chinese scholars. Before this, the China Cantos were effectively closed to the profane; there existed a stratosphere of arcane argument among great sinologists – Achilles Fang, P.H. Fang – and then there were the pioneering amateurs such as Hugh Kenner, Hugh Witemeyer, Donald Davie or Carroll Terrell in his *Companion*. Today, Roxana Preda, the force behind *The Cantos Project*, an ongoing, digital, fully annotated edition, is currently exploring Chinese aspects in some depth. Wenting Li from Sichuan and Lin Wei from Tianjin attempted to give an overview from the Chinese perspective. Their approach was described by Jeffrey Twitchell-Waas, himself a China hand and a serious scholar, as 'diplomatic', and when pushed a little, Wenting Li confirmed what one already suspected, that Pound's interests were eccentric and left-field, notably his choice of what to foreground; it was in no way the 'view' of history she was taught. Be it noted that nowhere in Pound is there any mention of Mao. Another expert remarked that the poet, who enjoyed drawing ideograms, never mastered the basic technique of 'stroke order' – it was all the curiosity of the amateur. As so often in Pound (*Propertius*, *Cathay*), 'productive misreading' seems part and parcel of his genius. Meanwhile, for his book *Ezra Pound's Japan*, the scholar Andy Houwen was awarded the annual Pound Society prize for best monograph.

The vexed question of Pound studies at the dawn of the AI era arose. Many furrowed brows and a lot of head scratching. Roxana Preda said she uses AI, but always 'follows up' to verify the information received. But I wondered, perhaps naively, how can one follow up a system that synthesizes a range of sources so vast it cannot be encompassed by one human mind? More furrowed brows and head scratching. Not to mention the question of intellectual property and copyright.

Talking of legal questions, Robert Spoo (scholar at Princeton and copyright lawyer) sketched out a rather daring theory that *Drafts & Fragments* in fact conceals a liminal critique of marriage (and monogamy) based on arcane 'property law'. Common to his practice of selecting what suited him, Pound's choices here were possibly dictated by personal circumstances. For the awkward fact is that when he arrived in Brunnenburg he was in love with his secretary, the Texan Marcella Spann, who accompanied him from the US, in a party that included his legitimate wife Dorothy. A love triangle (or even a quadrangle – for Mary's mother, Olga Rudge, was always hovering nearby on the fringes) was in place. Inevitably, Marcella was soon expelled by the other women, which undoubtedly contributed to the poet's growing depression. But Pound is never 'personal' in that sense; the *Drafts & Fragments* contain cadences and phrases which attain a universality in which the 'biographical' is winnowed or burned away.

And anyway, here comes Mary the dutiful daughter, assuredly a reconciling presence all these years, ferried across the courtyard in an antique lemon-yellow Fiat 500 that matches her dress, to a party at which she will be seen to dance. An iconic scene, from a film by Jean-Luc Godard. Speaking of which, the next EPIC was scheduled at the closing Business Meeting. It will take place in the summer of 2027, in Paris.

Set 11: Mondo de Virinoj kaj štormo

TRANSLATED BY JOHN GALLAS

1.
The March Wind

Maria Banuș (1914–1999)/Romania

There's a mad March wind in the turn of the world.
Today it has taken its turn with me.
I believe in the apples, round and ripe,
That will figure its pause and pregnancy.

The whole earth shakes. It shakes with life.
The March wind tumbles the turning sky.
We believe in the drive of newmade thoughts,
The startled *now,* and the scoured *I.*

The March wind howls in the turning world:
Believe in your strength. The trees are bare.
Invisible turbulence beats the branches.
Infinite darkness fills the air.

2.
Storm in a poppyfield

Regina Ullmann (1884–1961)/Germany

Once I walked in a poppyfield in a storm,
long ago –
and it was my dress,
red silk and wide as wide...
like satinwisp poppies upsidedown.
And a wheel of it spun off me and kept the field
from harm, all harm...
I was bade to that red field
to see a lovelier world,
that day, so long ago.

3.
Why dislike the wind...

Anonymous (twelfth century)/Japan

Why dislike the wind
that plucks at the trees?
Blossom is made to scatter.

Why shut my ears
to the storm-clatter of hail on the roof?
It is not my war.

Why look away
when driven cloud rags on the mountain peaks?
My heart is torn.

4.
The Dance of Sister Rain

Eugène Marais (1871–1936)/South Africa

Our Sister's dance. She eyes us, shy and breezy,
round the pike-tops. Chuckles. Asks with a hand.
Her armloops glitter, beads blink. She asks quietly.
Asks Wind to the raindance. The land is long.
The wedding looks wild.

Antelope thunder off the flats, crowd at the hilltops,
snouts pumping, gulping Wind, craning down
at her light spoors in the dust. The Littlemen under the ground
hear her feet pat past, climb closer, and sing:
Sister, Sister, you're here.

Her beads rattle. Legloops glint copper in the sunspin.
An eagle's firefeather sheets on her head: she walks
down from the pike-tops, folds out her grey blanket,
both arms wide – and Wind's breath breaks.
Our Sister's dance.

5.
Desolation

Gabriela Mistral (1889–1957)/Chile

The fog is thick and endless. Waves unmoor me,
wild, insistent, one after the other.
The dark land I have come to has no Spring:
but one long night that holds me like a mother.

Round my house the dark wind stamps its beat,
and wails, and shatters, glass-like, all my cries.
And down the long, white, unhorizoned plain,
I watch while sunset, mad with sadness, dies.

Who can she reach, who comes to this far place,
beyond beyond, where only deadmen are,
to stare upon a barren, silent sea,
with arms too weak to cross, and hope too far?

The ships with blanching sails that haunt the port
have come from lands where things are strange to me:
their flame-eyed men know not my riverpaths,
their pale fruits come not from my orchard-tree.

The questions rising in my throat grow dumb
upon their passing, past recovery:
they speak strange tongues unlike the simple songs
my mother, in the gold-lands, sang to me.

I watch the snow fall down like dust on bone;
I watch the fogmist bloat like dying men,
and see no time to not go mad in: thus
the long night now and now begins again.

I watch the rapt, wide plain, and catch its grief,
that comes to see the deathly landscape die:
snow is the face that peers into my glass:
eternal whiteness dropping from the sky.

Forever that; the silence of God's look,
his orangeblossom stare, the awful fate
that neither comes nor goes, upon my house,
falling, fierce and thrilling, while I wait.

Notes:
1. Maria Banus - new, with Cris Constantinescu.
2. Regina Ullmann – from *52 Euros*. Slightly amended.
3. Anonymous – new.
4. Eugène Marais – from *The Song Atlas*. Relined.
5. Gabriela Mistral – from *This Far Place* (SLG Press).

With thanks to Cris Constantinescu, Phoebe Ravenhall, H. Ishino.

Letter from Tartu

PENNY BOXALL AND REBECCA WATTS

Imagine a leafy, sparsely populated city with abundant birdlife and great coffee shops, where national pride manifests freely in the form of widespread respect for the environment and enthusiastic attendance at literary-cultural events. If you've lived mainly in England and are reading *PNR*, this probably sounds like Utopia. Alighting in the pristine, largely empty airport in Tallinn after a delayed flight from Dante's *n*th circle (aka London Luton), you can be forgiven the cognitive dissonance you experience walking by the airport café (cosily furnished with bookshelves, standard lamps and sheepskin rugs) and along the glass exit/entrance corridor (tastefully flanked by quotations from the country's great contemporary composer). 'Love is the source of all arts. Art exists as long as the ability sto love exists.' Welcome to Estonia.

From the spotless public coach (equipped with free hot drinks machine) we watch woodland and farmland roll by on either side of the road. We spy storks nesting in the tops of pines. We think we glimpse (in retrospect unlikely) a lone wolf loping across a field. We are destined for Tartu, Estonia's second city, to take part in the annual Prima Vista literary festival.

[PB: My association with Tartu began in the summer of 2022, when I applied for a month's residency through the UNESCO Cities of Literature network and quickly fell in love with this compact, romantic, quiet university town. Since then I've returned to Estonia a dozen times, in one capacity or another – to other festivals, for collaborations, and for a madcap makeshift residency on the remote island of Ruhnu. There's everything to love about Tartu: its clean, eminently swimmable river, the Emajõgi; its fade-coloured wooden houses in districts called things like Soup Town; and – above all – its commitment to literature. It matters here, and nowhere is that more evident than during May's international festival.]

[RW: I have no prior association with Tartu, or with Estonia. I'm just tagging along with Penny. Once I've met her at Luton I am in her hands.]

Prima Vista has an inventive and joyful approach to books. Marja Unt, assisted by a team, oversees the programming, which is predictable only in its excellence. This year there's a palpable sense of the connections established and being forged with other UNESCO Cities of Literature (and other generally 'literary' cities), and between participants at the festival. There's also a strong sense of the collegiate – something approximating a high-culture freshers' week. The festival's performers hail from Estonia, Latvia, Lithuania, Finland, Germany, Denmark, the Netherlands, Cuba, Japan and the UK. Everyone speaks brilliant English in addition to their native language(s). As invited guests we're treated to a traditional Hanseatic barge cruise up and down the Emajõgi, a festive dinner at a local Armenian/Georgian restaurant, a beautiful goody bag filled with books, notebooks and handcrafted chocolates, and (naturally) a certificate from Tartu's mayor commending and thanking participants for their valued contributions. It's all so welcoming and dignified. There is nothing apologetic about it, and nothing flashy or self-conscious either. In all the interactions brought about by the festival, there is a deep and nuanced appreciation of language: not merely as the basis for literature, but as a valuable channel that connects us with our distinctive cultural heritages, and a tool for finding common ground.

On our first evening in Tartu (the festival has been in full swing for three days already) we make our way to the German Cultural Institute for a discussion and readings by current writers-in-residence Julia von Lucadou and Ernesto Salazar-Jiménez. The room is almost full when five of us from the UK arrive and take seats in the front row. Realising that we won't be able to understand if the event proceeds in German, the panel suggests switching to English, knowing the rest of the (majority Estonian) audience can manage with that. A vibrant discussion follows, with the Estonian host Kai Aareleid switching between German and English, and the guest writers kindly and playfully assisting one another to relay their nuanced responses through Spanish and German into English. In the high-ceilinged, rococo interior of the Institute, it's a refreshingly human experience. When the writers read from their novels and poems (in German) we close our eyes or follow along on the handout, relaxing into their rhythms, with just the occasional jolt of a recognised word or phrase. We have to leave after ninety minutes to participate in another event, but the rest of the audience remains keenly attentive and genuinely engaged.

The audiences at all the (free) events we attend are strong and varied. At an afternoon workshop with Danish writer-in-residence Helene Grøn, a mixture of local students and international writers genially squish onto cushions on the floor of the Fahrenheit 451° Book Room, which occupies an alcove of a lively restaurant space within the Aparaaditehas (a former Soviet widget factory, since transformed into a 'cultural factory'). Competing with the noise from the restaurant, we share imaginary maps of our childhood hangouts with strangers from other countries. We miss some of each other's meanings and it doesn't matter; we feel we've travelled, in memory and in conversation, by the time we leave. Another workshop, this time in Tartu's Literature House with the UK-based writer Andy Willoughby, sees a motley band of participants marching as one up and down the banks of a paper river, dredging up vocabulary and discarded objects from the waterways and languages of our own experience.

On a series of writer-led walks we move through the city's parks, suburbs and neglected edgelands in search of nightingales, hedgehogs, saints and extra-terrestrial energies: some real, some fabled, all conjured or enlivened by the commissioned contributions of our imaginative literary guides. At the end of one such walk, which has taken a group of sixteen strangers three kilometres out of the city centre to a residential street named *Siili* (Estonian for hedgehog), an American-sounding audience member announces that he and his West Highland Terrier will now perform a series of tricks for our amusement. Everyone sticks around to watch, because we're a group now and why not? It's all very organic and eccentric, in an uncliched, unpretentious way, which we think is made possible by the festival's genuinely cross-cultural outlook. It's hard to imagine the same spontaneity and good humour flourishing at an equivalently funded literary festival in the UK.

Dispersing from the walks, and between events, we gather troupes of friends old and new, serendipitously finding the perfect café for that afternoon's discussion, with space enough for all of us once the occupants have jovially budged up and invited us to share their tables. Yes, the people in the café have also been enjoying the festival. A bunch of strangers re-enacting a hedgehog-summoning chant in English barely raises an eyebrow. Despite the exhaustion that comes with attending back-to-back events and walking many kilometres each day, we feel we could stay far beyond our allocated four days. We feel that perhaps this is our life now: weaving in and out of literary performances and animated chats with new friends from distant lands; learning to coexist with languages we can't yet understand.

For the festival finale we head back to the Literature House (now furnished with a DJ and disco lights) for a compelling performance in Latgalian – a language from eastern Latvia with little over 150,000 speakers – from award-winning 'rap princess' ŪGA and her close-harmony girls' group juos īluos līluos. The programme tells us that 'the group was formed as part of a project dedicated to the legacy of Latgalian poet Seimaņs Putāns. After their initial collaboration and joint songwriting, the ensemble decided to continue making music together.' Also: 'The concert is free of charge. Everyone is invited to experience Latgalian rap!' Neither us nor the many locals who've responded to the invitation know what's being said, but rhythm and attitude are universal languages and the majority of us are on our feet. It's a fitting end to a festival whose purpose is to celebrate the joys and surprises of performative language.

Wistfully awaiting our flight home, we conclude that literature isn't dead. It lives in Tartu.

Letter from Wales

SAM ADAMS

Lord, when they kill me, let the job be thorough
And carried out inside that county borough
Known as Merthyr, in Glamorganshire,
A town easy enough to cast a slur
Upon, I grant. Some cyclopean ball
Or barn-dance, some gigantic free-for-all,
You'd guess, had caused her ruins, and those slums –
Frightening enough, I've heard, to daunt the bums...

Thus Glyn Jones in a love letter (though you might not suspect that) to his birthplace. Perhaps with an outing in prospect, I bought the Landranger 160 'Brecon Beacons/Bannau Brycheiniog' Ordnance Survey map, probably soon after it was reprinted in 1996. Spread out, it promises well-scattered villages, a couple of small towns and as much high, open country as you could wish to view in in a day – apart from the bottom right-hand corner, which is largely occupied by the urban-industrial sprawl, here a relative term, of Merthyr Tydfil, current population 58,000. The town's name celebrates the martyrdom of Tydfil, one of the many daughters of the legendary fourth-century king Brychan Brycheiniog, who gives his name to the mountains and the neighbouring county. About the middle of the nineteenth century it was boasted to be the 'iron capital of the world'.

Close examination reveals a minor road leading east from the town centre, through Twynyrodyn, where, as we know from Meic Stephens's poem, half wild mountain ponies would come down to the streets in winter for shelter and hand-outs. Thereafter the road dwindles, climbing and narrowing, past Ffos-y-Fran ('Crows' Ditch') before splaying out in minor routes over the moorland, mostly a thousand feet or more above sea level. The map indicates spoil heaps and extensive, unnaturally-shaped pools between these tracks that are probably evidence of earlier mining activity. That would have been deep mining via shafts sunk vertically or levels slanting downwards to deep coal seams, the familiar patterns in the Valleys. Where the mines were successful and productive, they invariably littered the landscape with prominent, even colossal, heaps of pit waste, often mixed with ashes from the boilers that supplied steam power. Given time, this combustible combination could produce a simulacrum of low-level volcanic activity. Gilfach Goch had a fine example under the main (only) road around the valley, which emitted clouds of smoke and, especially when it rained, an evil stench. The mines closed. What coal remained deep underground stayed there, and the tips stayed on the surface. There was no suggestion, or at least none acknowledged, that previous mine owners, or the NCB, should remove them. In more recent times, however, they have been greatly diminished, if not erased, by the plunder of this slag, often conveniently burned to coke *in situ*, to provide hardcore for building projects. That put money in the pockets of the enterprising few and advanced the notion of the greening of the Valleys towards reality.

Over time, deep mining left prominent and long-lasting scars on the landscape. The footprint of open-cast mining falls more suddenly and, depending on the extent of the readily exposed seam of coal, best imagined as a thick, black blanket stretched over a wide area, can be of an altogether greater order of magnitude. A decade after my OS map was printed, a business was set up to extract coal from the upland area of Ffos-y-Fran by open-cast mining. Work on the extensive site was continuing in May 2023. You do not need to go there to see the effect of this kind of industrial activity, for the computer will present you with a vision of Ffos-y-Fran as an endlessly churning black hell infested by tiny mechanical insects – actually enormous hydraulic dump-trucks. But lessons have been learned. Once the trucks would have hauled their loads along public roads, as I well remember from the time when the tips in Gilfach were being removed, but here the bulk of the coal is taken to a Welsh Government railhead a couple of miles east of Merthyr for transport via a freight-only line to Cardiff and onward distribution. These arrangements are a vast improvement on those that prevailed in the previous history of coal mining in South Wales, though in a distant echo of the careless free-for-all of the past, coal extraction at Ffos-y-Fran continued several months after the closure date declared by the Welsh Government.

The latest episode in the history of Merthyr Tydfil has been far less turbulent and bloody than those of the past. The town will always be associated with the major part it played in the Industrial Revolution in the eighteenth century, when the proximity of both coal and iron ore facilitated the founding by enterprising incomers, notably the Crawshays, originally from Yorkshire, and the Guests, from Shrewsbury, of what were at the time the largest ironworks in the world. Some may recall it was at the Penydarren Ironworks in Merthyr that Richard Trevithick created a steam engine, initially to power an industrial hammer, and by mounting it on wheels created the first steam locomotive. What comes most readily to my mind when I think of Merthyr is not its often rough-and-tumble contribution to industrial history, or the 'Merthyr Rising', or even the tragic story of Dic Penderyn, but two writers who were born there, Glyn Jones (1905–1995), whose poem begins this piece, and Leslie Norris (1921–2006). Both were teachers, Leslie finally at Brigham Young University, Utah, and greatly admired and honoured as poets and short story writers. They were, too, both gentle and genial men: we miss them still.

FROM THE ARCHIVE

from PNR 185, vol. 35, no. 3
January – February 2009

Of the Beloved Someone

Christopher Middleton

Contributors to the issue included
Carola Luther, Adam Thorpe,
Chris McCully and Stephanie Burt

Confused about that which
Touches nothing, without which
There would have been nothing,

Attend to it a moment,
Attend: as it retrieves,
On this day like no other,

A joy, once to have felt in it
Nothing to be acknowledged,
From an impact uplift, at the utmost

[...]

Writings for Brear

HORATIO MORPURGO

The children, asleep in the back after a 4 am start, aren't missing much. Dawn is cloud-cover filling slowly and greyly with light. Driving west across Cornwall, the A30 grows each year a little straighter here, wider there. The ferry this time batters and bludgeons its way through a heavier sea than normal. Passengers bend double, recklessly, voluptuously abandon themselves to being ill. I disappear into my binoculars, see no dolphins, am stoical. Waves foam and pitch, cross-hatched with the annual flickering of shearwaters.

Every August we do some (generally more pleasurable) version of this. The ship between Penzance and the Isles of Scilly is still the same one I first boarded about the age my son is now. I liked one island straight away. To describe Bryher as England's westernmost settlement makes it sound too bleak. Tresco, to its east, lies across a sheltered strait, more or less a sandy lagoon. The sea to its north and west, by contrast, is indeed jagged with rocks all the way to the horizon. The rest of the island group is to the south.

The Godolphin Report of 1579 takes up the story: 'The Isle of Treskawe with som others... did belong unto the Abby of Tavistocke, it is said that Mr Christopher Coplestone canne show writings for the isle called Brear... The auncient rents I know not but if any were paid they were but puffyns or like small value.' Puffins still pay the rent, after a fashion, or are a chief attraction of the 'wildlife tours' which carry visitors, weather permitting, in brightly coloured launches to those rocks and uninhabited islands out on the horizon.

Exactly four centuries after Godolphin reported, a dedicated teacher brought a small group of pupils here on a school trip. It made at least one of them a birdwatcher for life. He badgered his parents to book a holiday on Bryher, as now his own children badger him.

The ferry docks at Hugh Town, on the main island of St Mary's. The pavements of its high street are agreeably solid this year. An open-air production of *The Tempest* is advertised. We add it to the long and greedy to-do-list with which we always begin our week here. What we have just sailed through was, it turns out, the leading edge of an actual tempest which arrives later, after we have transferred to our destination.

There, we have more or less slept off the early start when through thin walls familiar intonations are detectable. We don't have Netflix at home so sibling rivalries sharpen as soon as we go anywhere. Especially the first evening. We settle in the end on something with an environmental theme. Heavy rain drums and the wind gusts. I am dimly aware, as we watch, that it has been drumming and gusting for some time. It takes a lightning flash and a rumble in rapid succession, though, before we finally pause our choice and go to the window. We start paying belated attention to what is going on while we slumber here.

The entire archipelago and the sky above it have turned different shades of the same dim green-gold. As if the islands had all been recast in bronze. This was more like a transmutation than a weather event. What could be behind it? Is this the kind of light which warns, in the tropics, of a hurricane's approach? As if something has slipped an apocalyptic filter across the sun's disc: it feels closer to an eclipse than anything else.

By the time I reach the top of the island, the tempest is a dark receding smudge, but still taking up most of the eastern sky. Over the western horizon hangs a calm glow: maybe that eerie earlier light was created by horizontal rays from the sun as it set, passed through a downpour. Such explanations feel inadequate to the sheer strangeness of our welcome.

One-off special effects notwithstanding, I experience every year a low-level anxiety about this trip. Is it really planet-saving defiance of Easy Jet and all its works that brings us here? Or is this merely a symptom of slowdown, of laziness disguised as loyalty? Are we opposing to the instant gratification of cheap flights some slower principle of growth? Or fixating on our lucky, limited corner of the planet, because it is *our* corner?

Well, we have a week each year to buy in groceries and work it out all over again. After that freakish start, everything goes back politely inside the parameters of normal. Rock pools are unaffected by fog. The heron on its pond is indifferent to drizzle.

You can march around Bryher in a couple of hours. Lots of people do, though the qualities of the isle may not reveal themselves to that kind of examination. I've often watched the early morning transatlantic jets flying in, for all I know already on their descent into whichever European city it will be. All those options. I'm reluctant to fly but most 'slow travel' is premised on the kind of time and money almost nobody has. So what about its less thoroughly written-up relation, then, namely travelling hardly any distance?

That is what we generally now do. Sea anemones. Open-air Shakespeare. It can feel terminally quaint, like playing at 1860. Or isn't there a place, I'll argue back, then, for places where the present has not swept all before it? Doesn't anywhere you take the trouble to know well eventually begin to open up this question? I reproach myself on bad days with falsifying this place, with trying to bring it to a halt. The mood usually, thankfully, passes and the unfairness with it.

Paul Goodman long ago both ironised and admired 'the courage with which we human beings soon root ourselves in a new home, in an unlikely place, and decorate the place, and are patriotic once more'. We 'decorate' Bryher this year with, among other things, our first dahlia anemone crowned with several rings of brilliant white tentacles. But I've done something like this for as long as I can remember. I 'decorated' the whole of the West Country as a child, after our move there, by making myself encyclopaedic about birds and Elizabethan explorers. With rocks and ocean all around, with an intrepid sea journey to reach them, the Scillies were readily co-opted.

I didn't then know about the Godolphin Report, which puts it like this: 'Within the circyt of these isles are sundry good Roades [i.e. anchorages] and Harborows for shippes veary commodious and needfull unto divers her majisties subjects and neighbours... As for the harmes that would ensew if any enemy should achieve [i.e. occupy] the same I judge myself unsufficient to [unfold]...' Read this and the remains of sixteenth-century fortifications here cease to be blankly stared-at end-points of after-supper walks. Their presence begins instead to make more sense, to feel less 'unlikely'. Yours too, even.

There is more to this. Ships venturing into the Atlantic before the eighteenth century had to rely on latitude, measured from the height of the sun or pole star. The 50th parallel was the most convenient for English vessels to follow. Because Scilly lies so close to it, the islands often occupy a special place in accounts of voyages, either as the last sailors saw of England when they left or the first of it they saw upon their return.

Carl Schmitt began his story of 'unencumbered technology' with the ocean-going vessels used by early modern explorers. Life on such ships, he argued, was life more absolutely reliant on technology than it ever had been before. The technology was 'unencumbered' because its application was no longer embedded in society, as technological innovation on land must still be. Its users were 'liberated' from the kind of ethical precepts which might have held them in check at home. How thoroughly they explored and exploited this 'liberty' of theirs haunts us yet. Schmitt saw here, and surely he was right, technology striking out on a new path, dispensing in a new way with the past.

Their astrolabes, quadrants and compasses may be remote ancestors of the on-board computers which guide today's aircraft to their destinations. But the line of descent is direct. The technology now tracking and directing us everywhere did not come from nowhere. Its spirit long preceded the invention of computers. The first accurate survey and mapping of these islands, as we'll see, were unintended by-products of a sixteenth-century expedition to China. I well recall my astonishment at this discovery, as I added it to the store of everything Scilly has meant and still means now.

We make the most of clear skies one morning and hire kayaks, paddling to a nearby uninhabited island. Samson is famous for the cowrie shells that wash up on the blazing white of its beaches. Tradition has it that if you find one you'll come back. It appeals to me that such a decision is said to depend on a small thing that is quite difficult to see. On some days, especially when you find one, the tradition feels true to a secretive something about this place, the same something that is lost on those who march around one island before lunch, then another launch, and then another island. On other days, especially when you don't find one, this 'tradition' feels more like the astute invention of a guesthouse owner.

Today it is the former. The tide is right out, sand flats exposed, and I am in luck. Pocketing this year's finds and their message, I become aware also of being shadowed by a flock of birds. Sanderlings are small waders, almost white, almost silver in some lights, as if they took their colouring from the beaches here. A favourite of mine on those early visits.

All twenty or thirty of them scarper before each breaking wave, then turn as one to pursue the same wave back down the beach. As if set to track forever the exact, shifting point where sea and land meet. A work-shy party now breaks away and heads toward me. Standing barefoot in my private pool of solar-heated water, I watch them encountering similar pools themselves. Three or four promptly start bathing so vigorously it looks more like a water fight. They leave behind a few feathers on the water. One of those is on my desk as I write.

A few are in summer plumage: their numbers around Scilly rise in August because the islands are a stop-over between the Russian Arctic or Greenland, where they breed, and their winter range around the Mediterranean. It's their small experience of humans which makes them so trusting. I like that about them, too, and the thought of where it comes from.

At the maximum extent of ice cover, around 24,000 years ago, a single glacier stretched from the mountains of what is now Wales across to the east coast of what is Ireland. Part of its southern rim ran across the northern edge of Scilly – Bryher's northerly half was buried under it. Sea-level was then 120m lower than today and the view from here was mainly of a colossal ice-flow. The glacier carried with it rocks and pebbles from hundreds of miles to the north. These 'erratics', left behind when it retreated, still occur on beaches here.

Today's temperate Europe was then tundra. The staggering distances covered by migratory birds today are traceable to that time. As the ice retreated, breeding grounds on that tundra edged every year a fraction farther off from winter feeding ranges. Each year the birds must travel a little further between them until they were travelling, as they do now, thousands of miles. The migration of sanderlings evolved in response to this change.

To be put in mind of such timescales then becomes in turn part of why you go back. The erratic flint which tells you how far south the ice extended then. A few birds picking their way along the shore can fill you in on its present whereabouts. Are we and our personal timescales mere trifling intruders in this landscape, mere 'erratics'? Yet they persist in mattering and why should they not? That twelve-year-old, forever peering through binoculars into the middle distance, inevitably missed a good deal. He has tried to make up for it since but the Irish Sea Glacier, for all its thousands of square miles and billions of tonnes, sometimes feels like a relatively small part of what he didn't know.

To the man he has grown into, the Scillies seem a 'smarter' destination than they were. A decade before his first visit, a Labour leader could signal his commitment to Everyman by holidaying here. A pair of binoculars round your neck once signalled membership in a sort of benign masonry. Good binoculars don't have to be expensive and knowledge about wildlife can be acquired pretty much for free and at any age. The social levelling came built-in and was a part of what I always liked about it.

On a recent visit, the passenger next to me in a launch had a pair round his neck. So I asked, seventies style, if he'd seen anything interesting. He looked me up and down: 'Not really', he answered. 'I *did* see the Duchess of Cambridge', he went on. '*That* was interesting.' I searched his expression for an ironic glimmer. All I could find, if I'm not mistaken, was a hint of spite.

I hesitate to draw the obvious inference. The Scillies have not escaped the wider gentrification of Cornish tourism. Confirmed sightings of film stars grow more frequent. But is it really the world that has changed? Because the Royals have a fan? Or rather that I see it now with clearer eyes? Both, both, knowledge, self-knowledge. Each visit adds to a kind of sedimentary formation in which layers of the personal, historic and prehistoric alternate. Upheavals of every kind leave their trace. Bryher's northern hills scarred by the weight of ice. The cottage we stay in built for flying boat crews stationed here during the war.

The first accurate map of Scilly is a good example, drawn just as human restlessness finally caught up with the sanderlings'. John Davis undertook three voyages in search of a route to China in the 1580s. He discovered instead the strait between Greenland and the Canadian Arctic which is still named after him. But setting out on the first of those voyages, in July 1585, bad weather detained him on Scilly. His ships, *The Sunshine of London* and *The Moonshine of Dartmouth*, were tied up for two unscheduled weeks in a little port on Treskawe, directly opposite Brear.

New Grimsby is still watched over by the ruins of the fort which guarded it then. Strategic concerns, as we've seen, were keenly felt in 1579 and rightly so. Within a decade the Spanish Armada did indeed aim to rendezvous off Scilly and only the weather prevented it. The archipelago is noticeably absent from the maps of England which William Saxton drew and published between 1574 and 1579. Davis therefore used his fortnight, his fly-boat and the instruments brought along for New World discoveries, to accurately survey and map these islands for the first time.

Davis was born in Devon but lived for some years at Mortlake, in the home of John Dee, the Queen's advisor on maritime exploration. Dee instructed him there in the use of his 'paradoxal compass', later described by his pupil as an 'instrumēt portable, of easie stowage and small practise'. The compass was Dee's proudest achievement, but his account of exactly what it was and what it did is lost. It was some kind of navigational aid for explorers in the higher latitudes. First invented for earlier missions to the Russian Arctic, also in search of a route to China, Davis would certainly have had one on board with him here.

Dee was a significant presence at court and deeply versed in many branches of the new learning. A figure of daunting complexity, he was a mathematician, kabbalist and an alchemist at a time when boundaries between religion, emergent science and the occult were notoriously blurred. He is widely regarded as an inspiration for Shakespeare's Prospero.

Which brings us to that poster of which we had taken note on arrival. The week is usually half gone before we begin to make serious inquiries about our plans. *The Tempest*, though, looked as if it might come to something: the play would transfer to Tresco on our last evening, for its final performance on Scilly. The launch booked to carry the cast back to St Mary's afterwards could drop us on Bryher. It only remained now to arrange for the right weather.

A bundle of hangings embroidered with strange emblems was visible in the storage area as we crossed to Tresco earlier that day. A long and curiously carved staff lay nearby. Looking about us on the crowded boat, I tried to guess which the actors were. They were none of them film stars so I couldn't, but that only added to the strangeness.

After picnicking on a beach, there was plenty of time to disagree over which footpath led to the ruined fort. When the wind picked up, we took refuge in a pub and read. Towards evening, though, the sky cleared and the wind dropped. The play was to be performed in the Tropical Gardens, which are extensive. Unsure of the exact venue, I went ahead with my son to locate it. Wandering through the exuberant vegetation, a young man we met introduced himself as Ferdinand and showed us the way.

Having seen a couple of film versions and read it as a graphic novel, my son was keen to try out his ideas. The play was surely too harsh on Caliban, he maintained: 'This island's mine by Sycorax my mother'. Caliban was born there. Everybody else leaves at the end. If the island is anyone's, it's his, surely. Prospero is an intruder. What did Ferdinand think?

I walked behind, texting our whereabouts while I eavesdropped. Is Caliban's insistence upon his right to the island, it occurred to me now, an early example of 'survivance'? It's a term for the many forms indigenous resistance can take – 'an active sense of presence over absence, deracination and oblivion... the continuance of stories...'. I wondered further, as I eavesdropped: why does my son home in on this time after time?

Caliban was probably inspired as much by the 'wild man' of European folklore as by anyone encountered by the explorers. Gerald Vizenor, the Native American writer who first used 'survivance' in this sense, calls Caliban the 'great white mongrel' in his fiction, as if to acknowledge his European heritage, but also includes him among indigenous story-tellers. Does any ten-year-old, I reflected now, especially one strongly connected to a place, share in a kind of faith? Is he, through that faith, already aware intuitively of an outside world that will seek to requisition that place, and him, for use as a backdrop to its own dramas?

We are the first of the audience to arrive where the stage is set and the cast is gathered, chatting. Rows of chairs stand empty. Ferdinand turns to me with a quizzical look: it appears I have run up some vicarious credit. So I ask whether he knows about Tresco's *Tempest* connection, tell him about Dee as inspiration for Prospero, as a trainer of sea pilots. He wears a 'curiouser-and-curiouser' expression as I tell him of one such pilot, departing for China, as he hoped, from a stone quay not twenty minutes' walk from where we are standing.

Take as many years as you need with a place, build up all the associations you like. Communicating their charm may be less straightforward than you imagine. I finish my summary and watch Ferdinand hesitate. He is about to say something tactful. And then he does.

'I'm – er – not sure I'd be able to repeat all that and do it justice but Prospero, as it happens, is right behind you...'

I turn and the Duke of Milan smiles absently, pleased with being mentioned and wanting to be polite, but sticking for now with the conversation he already has. The director just then calls on them all to get into costume. Prospero and his future son-in-law excuse themselves and so the chance to deliver my message to the 'personified type of the creative' melts into air, into thin air.

The weather is with them and they play to a full venue. To enter his world of Magian invention, the exiled Duke has only to thump the ground once with that staff which had accompanied us in the boat from Bryher. Once again, his project gathers to a head. His charms crack not and in no time Antonio and Alonso stand 'spell-stopped' as he moves among them, recalling, convicting, forgiving.

In this production they stand motionless, give no outward sign of hearing. To whom, then, or to what is he speaking in that scene? To their consciences? To their unconscious or past selves? Is Prospero Magus, priest, psychoanalyst, neurodivergent? What kind of words are they that truly reach the hearer, as Prospero's reach Antonio in that scene?

A cast of travelling players, at the mercy of Cornish weather, bringing with them the simplest props and scenery, prove as well able to prompt such questions as any better-funded outfit. They are still humming about mine ears as we walk afterwards to the quay, Brear's silhouette ablaze with the sun going down behind it and with everything that play has meant.

Our wait for the ferry on St Mary's, the following day, would have been quite different had we not seen that play. Queuing to buy sea sickness tablets, I would not have seen Prospero waiting at the entrance to the supermarket, then walking towards the main square with Alonso. None of us would have seen Ariel returning from his solitary stroll along the coast path with an old-fashioned cine camera.

The sea sickness tablets are unneeded. Our return crossing is calm. Watching Gonzalo and Antonio disembark together at Penzance, our revels are not quite ended and neither are our travels. We break the journey home with a day or two where my parents live in the Devon countryside. Arriving well past eleven, we carry luggage in exhausted silence from the car to a silent house. Once everything is in, I go to a north-facing window and look out.

There's a chance the *aurora borealis* will be visible even this far south tonight. All the time I was growing up in this house we never saw it. But that band of light along the northern horizon surely cannot be Bideford, unless it has grown meanwhile into a far mightier conurbation than the one I knew. Those two upright beams of light, for example – or are my eyes imperfectly adjusted to something? Even as I watch they are gone.

I lead my family by a promise, native here, back out under the stars. They are roughly half-convinced as we come to the gateway beyond which is a field with a clear view north. Whatever there is, if it is there at all, is sure to be visible from the top of it. A cut of sileage has just been taken and a smell of cut grass hangs in the air. Craning our heads back as we walk, we gaze up at night skies as dazzling as ever they were.

From the brow of that hill it is beyond question. Two, now three columns of blue-green radiance have unmistakably risen up out of that glow along the horizon that can't be Bideford. My family believes me now. A pair of headlights turn a corner on the far side of the valley, appear ludicrously small then vanish, as if for scale. And many many were those, to judge by what was later posted online, who gladly accepted this invitation from the cosmos to explore night mode on their androids. Many cool pics uploaded.

Meanwhile that play is still running in my head: how would a Caliban have conjured by this midnight phosphorescence? How tricked it into revealing the secret, sacred story of how our world was brought to birth? To a Dee/Prospero, what would this have been if not a vivid manifestation of astral influence? An angelic communiqué insensible to the profane. The living signature appended to a letter from the universe.

If some such power to attend as Shakespeare could assume in his audience is lost or at risk, what practises might revive or strengthen it? Or how might a successor to it be found? If we cannot be reached by this, spell-stopped on our hill-tops, what words of Prospero or anyone else will ever reach us? There was even a meteor shower thrown in – one of them flew clean through the aurora as we watched. Mere matter hurtling to inevitable disintegration, or a heavenly messenger sent to blaze one final trail?

We must not mind too much, I think, how old-fashioned or idiosyncratic the answers we give to such questions seem to others. The columns fade, from three to two, back to none. We walk to the house and to our beds, another week on Scilly added to the store. As each past visit was present this year, so will this one be a presence next time. What the places I know best incrementally teach me, through these repeat visits, forms the core of my answer.

Three Poems

CAROL RUMENS

Unlovely, but

not always... I remember
when some con-artist of the harp or lyre
played back to me the beauty of my guess,
and I was found, or suddenly emergent,
in streets of ritual fire
where leaping kids get burned by happiness.

I was an alien there:
the enemy-sisters powder-blushed their cheeks,
played *caring*. It was social politics...
But was it? Rules go west, I thought, when war
makes the light touch, the small-talk, heavier,
and heads – some heads – are lost when kindness speaks.

Even formalist poets ditched reticence.
Crash the boundaries. Out with pretence!
Do as you dream... they slapped a rainbow-new
strip-magnet on the licence.
Take it as read – read LGBTQ...
No warning-signs darkened our leafy zoo.

Don't *Feed. Don't Touch.* I bump into the mirror,
a let-down drunk, repelled.
'I'd like to tear your face off, tear
your eyes, your mouth, your rotten fucking face off.'
I scrabbled fingernails at cheeks, jabbed glass
at wrists. (The blood-test failed.)

What should I name my sin?
I'd never thought I'd win
hearts from a rat-arsed rap with suicide.
There was no crafty scheme. Some fool phoned in.
He grassed me up. And even then, the dream
limped on, some look of hers hadn't quite died.

Are male same-sex-abusers also musers
on the exchange they 'knew' to be consensual?
Do they re-nerve it
in the un-pleasured leisure of the cell,
the damp bedsits, or boozers,
swearing their love, brain-aching to deserve it?

Age is the deep-mind mist that sighs *forget*,
but I could sometimes kill
that sickle-shouldering bore
haunting the coatless hall-way. Look, tonight
The table's set. Pink glows the Zinfandel.
The flesh I turned to stone walks through the door.

Taking Turns

Cry-for-it bread
leave-the-kids-in-the-bed
walk-miles-for-it bread

They walked miles
got there early
the queue massive.
They tried to join it
without moving.

Without moving
women whispered
    the old way
        of mix, knead, play-
          with-the-kids, see-it-rise
    finger-sticky bread.
More flour! slap it out
    on your palm. It was called –

taboon, it was baked –
    it was baked in clay
      and straw and the grid
        was a grid of hot pebbles
          the white rounds browned
    in a flash – wait your turn –
        freckled and sweet
        with zataar spice

        kissed like a face
    a child's face

mind-you-don't-burn-
your-fingers, not
mind-you're-not-shot-
in-the-belly-bread

With covered heads
they crouch, they chew
their sour teeth
gulp down the acids
memory leaves
thin in the self-
consuming hunger

boys and men
they used to smile at
push them aside
brace, grab
even each other

roaring for
the bags the bags –
the one bag –

for the flour
for the bread
for the waterless
for the ovenless
in the sweating tents
if they ever get there

Two brothers under
the shelling called
'crowd control'
fought, drew knives
slit arteries
died

for nothing, for
life, for death, for what
does it matter?
Leave the kids in the bed.

There goes the bread
shouldered away
by the running ones
with the famine-legs
and the leaking bag
the soldier flung

struggling   home
as night comes on   over burnt crusts
on foot, in carts   over still-hot pebbles
trundling   where?

    only one prayer
    was left in the ash

    'Is-ra-el,
  didn't you know

that what you cook
            you too must
              swallow?'

Checkpoint: Denial

So how did you travel here?
How much did you pay?
What's this forgery of a passport?

I was always here, the same cloud
over our first day's words, our last night's touching.
Some countries just disappear.

Will the red car will turn into the yard again
with that single childish 'beep'?
Will you still love the smell, the male power, of petrol?

Our road was closed, the car stretchered away.
Its power's still dying somewhere.

Let it die. Are you pretending
you're too old and wise to see the faces
of the coming years?

Time's staying home. Familiar things float
and bump tomorrow-ish corners.
They never get through.
That lip-stained cup, those old beltless trousers
are simpler now than when we gave them form –
and brought to them our shy ceremonial –
tender, asexual.

So you want permission to stay
and die in this cold country?

I've unpacked everything I want to keep.
What I never found, I've dreamt I found.
Only in isolation can a lover
walk through the gate to the sea, then up to the city
that's gold at night, along the grass that never
leaves the side of a small, grey, happy river.

A Quest for the *Camaldolese Grail* in the footsteps of Lynette Roberts

FRANCESCA BROOKS

The librarian in the purple blazer opens the large grey archive box on the desk in front of me. Instead of the stunning fourteenth-century illuminated manuscript I thought I had ordered, my eye moves over clinical glass vials filled with dust and fibres, slithers of animal glue, nail fragments, splinters of wood, neat boxes labelled as 'remnants' of 'band ends' and 'head bands', sewing threads and sample materials, and a Perspex folder of cannibalised strips of leather. This box carefully itemises the detritus removed from the manuscript during its restoration in 2009. In place of a manuscript, a box of relics and fragments surviving from the manuscript's collapse, its assisted disintegration.

Do all manuscript restorations involve the careful archiving of dirt and waste material encountered in the process? This is not a manuscript, but its visceral remains; an archival reliquary box for the absent body of the manuscript, once crafted from the flayed skin of an animal. The librarian in the purple blazer is a little taken aback – 'Oh', she says.

Before I arrived at the National Visual Arts Library in the Victoria and Albert Museum, there was nothing I was more afraid of than this: being exposed as the sort of medievalist who doesn't know how to work with manuscripts. The sort of medievalist who would, for example, order the restoration box and not the manuscript. I have been waiting, expecting, to be denied access, either at the point of request or the point of arrival, and at multiple points along the way as I got lost in the V&A's galleries of decorative silverware, in the hushed corridors of illuminated stained glass panels and decadent displays of jewellery and tea sets. But the librarian's shock and her candour put me at ease, and I confess that this isn't what I expected either.

In this moment of mutual embarrassment, the librarian leaves to see if she might be able to order the right item and I am left with this curious box that both *is* and *is not quite* the manuscript I had hoped for.

I have come to the Art Library to see the Italian manuscript known as the *Camaldolese Gradual*, following in the footsteps of the Argentine-born Welsh poet and writer Lynette Roberts (1909–1995). Although her poetry is not widely known today, in the 1940s and early fifties Roberts found her work championed by her friend and editor at Faber and Faber, T.S. Eliot, who saw in her experimental, startling writing 'an unusual gift for observation and evocation of scenery and place', as well as a distinctive music that was simultaneously ancient and modern. Lynette Roberts wrote about the *Camaldolese Gradual,* and the four months she spent studying it and the work of the Italian Renaissance artist Lorenzo Monaco, in a 1940 issue of the magazine known as *Life and Letters Today,* and a December edition of the Argentine newspaper *La Nación.*

Her article in *Life and Letters* had interested me for a long time as an example of Roberts's direct, material engagement with the culture of the Middle Ages, a period of history that also informs the complex texture of her poetry. How and when had Roberts, who in 1940 was living as a writer and a housewife in a small, rural village in Wales, spent four months with this manuscript? Why would *Life and Letters* – a journal of contemporary arts and culture owned by the novelist Bryher, with its own fascinating history and networks – publish a piece of scholarship on Italian Renaissance art? There was something mysterious and compelling about this piece of writing's very existence. Exploring this mystery led me to still vital questions about access and academic gatekeeping, and alternative ways of knowing and perceiving the world, both material and sensorial: the value, in other words, of claiming access.

When I finally found a copy of the magazine at the Central Library in Manchester, Lynette Roberts's article seemed to me to be a kind of fantasy piece. First, there was the fact that Roberts kept referring to the *Camaldolese Grail*, not *Gradual*, a moniker that I couldn't seem to find any record of: deepening both the mystery and my sense of suspicion. There was also a touch of Roberts's developing interest in historical fiction evident in her evocation of the monastery where the manuscript was produced as a space filled with 'a hum of bees and smell of herbs with the humdrum of voices and murmuring of prayers'. This reverie is where the article breaks off: 'So, we will leave him in the cool glade of the corridor, with music and twilight lowering the sun, just sitting, sitting, as dreaming monks do'.

Finally, a critical and scholarly assuredness is mixed with an attention to colour and form that is eccentric and fanciful. Roberts writes about mushroom shades and mole tones and pink blancmange rocks. She draws our attention to the lines on a lake which do not depict ice, although she might forgive us for thinking so, but as she describes them appear to curve 'like bleached seaweed, oriental eyelashes, or flayed wheat'. Arguing for why she thinks we see Lorenzo Monaco's hand in this ostentatious, gilded manuscript, she writes that '[t]he miniatures which I have studied have the same pink blanc-mange rocks, the dark polished trees, lined haloes, heavy eye-shadow, and drooping mouths terminating in small dots' of the paintings she has observed in the National Gallery. Roberts doesn't simply describe the manuscript. She uses her poet's eye to vividly evoke her aesthetic and material encounter with this sacred object, producing a surreal portrait of a book that seems to distort time under her gaze.

Yet the surreal quality of her writing here is of a piece with the inventive, high-energy approach to language found in her late modernist poetry – published by

Faber in the mid-twentieth century and by Carcanet in the twenty-first – where colour is also a vivid element in her multisensory poetic palette. In her prose poem 'Swansea Raid', which recounts the three nights of bombing raids on Swansea in 1941, the colours of the intimate, rural domestic world of the village of Llanybri become toxic, saturated by the disorienting proximity of war's destruction. Roberts bears witness to the bombings as 'A glade of magnesium waning to a distant hill', and observes 'A collyrium sky, chemically washed Cu.DH2'. The violence provokes an at first awesome and then sickening metamorphosis: 'the cows returning to their sheds wear hides of cyanite blue, their eyes GLINTING OPALS!', crowds stand 'puce', and Rosie, a familiar Llanybri character from Roberts's poetry and diaries, is 'bleached' by the terrifying light of the bombings.

The bombings don't just wreak destruction, but promise a corrupting, chemical legacy that recasts the familiar sights and sensations of this Welsh village. The poem was also first published in *Life and Letters Today* under the title 'From a New Perception of Colour: And I shall take as my Example the Raid on Swansea'. Roberts herself was a disrupting, exotic flash of colour in the Carmarthenshire countryside. As an outsider to the village, she wore a bright red cloak on her walks down the laneways to the coast and drank *mate* from a silver *bombilla* spoon, as in her native Argentina – affectations that saw her accused of being a spy during the war, as recounted in her poem 'Raw Salt on Eye'. In the piece on Lorenzo Monaco, it is the vibrant pigments of centuries past that jolt Roberts towards the invention of new language and imagery, at a time when her sensory perceptions were otherwise unstable and in flux.

In her essay, Roberts connects her off-kilter, poetic accounts of the manuscript's illuminations with prose that is thoroughly steeped in the language of scholarship on fourteenth-century Italian painters. Performing her scholarly credentials, she quotes Giorgio Vasari and Walter Pater, draws a line between Giotto and Fra Angelico, and proclaims her certainty about the manuscript's probable origins in the Monastery Santa Maria Degli Angeli at the hands of Lorenzo Monaco, a fact otherwise not established. 'That this Choir Book contains the hand of Lorenzo I have no doubt', she writes: '[t]o study one painter fully is to know his brush work, colouring, temperament, and detailed characteristics like a small child.' When I reread the piece on the train to London, I feel guilty about my initial perception of it as a flight of fancy. Perhaps what I had felt was a pang of jealousy. Who had given Roberts permission to write with such freedom and evident pleasure about an artefact that to my mind had the sacrosanct aura of the forbidden about it?

Still a little self-conscious in the grand, classical surrounds of the Art Library, I pore busily over the visceral remnants of the restored manuscript. I write out in pencil my own itemised list of the box's contents, replicating the one created by an archivist, and making my work with this unexpected archival object seem purposeful in the process:

A – filler collected from back board
B – sliver of wood from tunnel of head sewing station of upper board
C – dust/dirt collected from gutter margins
D – miscellaneous slithers of wood from back board
E – needle found in text block
F – bent nail shank
G – fragments of nail from tail edge of front board
H – fragments of nail from head edge of front board
I – fragments of nail from head edge of back board

I photograph each of the small glass vials. The glimpse of dirt and fluff and grime preserved within is mediated by text written directly onto the glass in blue felt pen. When I encounter the 'spine linings from a previous rebind' preserved in plastic, I have the unsettling sense that what I am looking at is a fabric vertebra. I draw a quick sketch of the pattern made by the wounded fabric in my notebook. In addition to the photographs and the sketch, I make my own brief notes about the aesthetics of what I'm encountering here: 'tiny fragments of red and blue thread, like something you might sweep from the corner of the stairs', 'bog oak colour and texture of spine linings', 'anatomy of a medieval manuscript'.

When the real manuscript arrives, nothing about what I have seen so far could have prepared me for its immensity. Two attendants wheel the new grey archive box out from the back room on a trolley. Everyone is nervous of its weight, its grandiosity; it imposes itself and requires three of us to move it from out of its box and onto the padded bookrest. It is studded by round-headed nails in its seventeenth or eighteenth-century binding that make it look like a solid wooden chest or casket, and which have impressed their weight into the dark foam protecting the manuscript's back when it rests in its grey archive box. With the book still closed, I take in its vast leather cover embellished with decorative metalwork and notice a small handwritten label pasted on the binding that reads: 'Camaldolese Grail'.

A gradual is a book that collects the musical items of the mass, including in this case, the Sanctorale, the Office for the Dead, the Common of the Saints and Several Martyrs, as well as lists of saints and feasts in liturgical order. As it turns out, 'grail' is also a Middle English word for a 'gradual', still in use well into the nineteenth century – not so fanciful after all.

Due to the mix-up in ordering, I have less time with the manuscript than I might have liked. In contrast to the laboured attention I gave to the dirt and dusty remnants, I find myself moving at speed through the pages of the *Gradual/Grail* in search of hammered gold scenes and abstract, floriated initials – looking for colour amidst the small coded flags and black diamonds of musical neumes that dance across the pages. My ability to read music is limited, more so when faced with medieval notation systems. Instead, I turn the all-capturing eye of my camera on the book, greedy and acquisitive, seeking to record more than language might in the short space of time that remains.

I find myself drawn to some of the miniatures that speak in a language I do recognise – that of Christian biblical stories and the symbolism of the saints. In the miniature of the Annunciation an angel bows to Mary. The angel's white gown is shadowed by touches of blue that seem to reflect the deep, rich swathes of Mary's royal blue cloak. The angel's sleeves are fringed with red tassels and bells, but it is the wings that fascinate me: pen strokes delineate the fine texture of the feathers, which are also layered in gradations of shades of blue and green. There's a kind of quiet flamboyance to the *Grail*'s angel. In another miniature, Mary Magdalene appears in a sparkling, golden mandorla, which is raised aloft by a crowd of bright orange souls whose wings flick upwards like tongues of fire. Her flowing golden locks cover her otherwise naked body, as is traditional in medieval depictions of Mary Magdalene. Dressed in a robe made from the hair with which she tenderly washed the feet of Christ, she looks like a glamorous pagan or werewolf borne out of the wilderness, her sexuality now sanctified by her acts of devotion to Christ.

I'm also pleased to spot a depiction of my favourite saint, Saint Margaret, standing on the back of a whiskered, defeated dragon, whose decorated tail is curled up like the furled fronds of a young fern. Margaret became the patron saint of childbirth, not because she had experienced it, but because she burst from the belly of a dragon miraculously unscathed after being swallowed whole by the beast. This miracle meant that prayers to Margaret were often written on birthing girdles: rolls of parchment that would have been worn during childbirth (some surviving examples still retain traces of birth fluids).

When the time comes to stop my work, a small crowd of curious library staff arrive to inspect the manuscript before it gets stored away again. Although the V&A Museum is a rich storehouse of medieval culture, from gold reliquary caskets in the shape of a variety of saint's body parts to elaborate carved ivories, the Art Library is a more contemporary space. It holds a reference collection on fine and decorative arts, alongside exhibition and auction catalogues, and rare artist books from the twentieth and twenty-first centuries. Many of the staff did not know that they had a book this old in their collection. Like me, they have never had this kind of intimate, material encounter with a medieval manuscript.

I use their interest as an excuse to stay with the book a little longer, enjoying their questions and excited fascination, which matches my own mingled sense of trepidation and inquisitiveness – a shared feeling (or worry) of not quite living up to the aura of this object. The colours are so bright that one of the assistants asks if it has been restored; a manuscript so old and so unfathomably vibrant that it looks uncannily like its imitation, a forgery. Or perhaps it simply challenges our sense of the passing of time and its ruination.

Standing with these women in shared curiosity, it occurs to me that Lynette Roberts's article on Lorenzo Monaco has given me permission to come and spend time with this manuscript. It is not necessarily just about the *Camaldolese Gradual/Grail* either. She has given me an excuse to do this thing that has come to feel off limits to me so many years into an early career as a researcher: to consult any manuscript from this period without feeling ashamed of what I don't know, of what I can only learn through encounter.

The V&A Art Library has made it relatively easy to get an appointment with this book, but this is not the case with all institutions that find themselves the official keepers of old and rare manuscripts, especially when it comes to those books that have gained prestige as examples of our cultural heritage. We know that touch was an important part of how some medieval users engaged with their books (rubbing at the image of a significant saint, for example), but this kind of intimate engagement is anathema to their preservation now. This *Camaldolese Gradual/Grail*, with its rounded, gothic bookhand, rich pigments and lavish use of gold, was probably touched by only the privileged few: intended to inspire awe at a distance in congregants who would see it glinting in the candlelight of the monastery, its colours thrumming in the half dark.

Although Roberts has given me the gift of permission, she was no stranger to being denied access herself, and she had passionate ideas about what access to culture and heritage should look like. In her diaries and in her correspondence, published as *Diaries, Letters, Recollections,* Roberts railed against barriers to knowledge established by academic institutions. Writing about Idris Bell, at one time a curator at the British Museum, and his refusal to let her access some books from the early seventeenth century, Roberts reflected: 'I disturbed him in his iron cage, no doubt he locked the gate twice after I had left him'. Bell was clearly not the only person who frustrated her attempts to do research, locking the physical and metaphorical gates: in a diary entry from 1945 she compared academics to 'antique dealers who want to sell their hidden treasure but are at the same time reluctant to do so, with the result that they soon turn into junk shops and crumble in their own parasitic fervour'. In the modern university the demands of marketisation, as well as the commercial interests of publishers and investors, vie for precedence with ambitions to make research open and accessible to all as part of the university's contribution to the public good. Often, these imperatives and ideals can feel irreconcilable.

Research was essential to Roberts's poetic process. In her heroic poem about the Second World War as experienced by women and civilians in rural Wales, *Gods with Stainless Ears* (1951), the notes genuinely deepen our understanding of the text rather than confounding us with obscure references. Denise Levertov, the British-American poet who wrote about an 'authentic source of myth in poetry' in her essay *The Sense of Pilgrimage*, would surely have classed Roberts alongside Robert Duncan, Charles Olson, Ezra Pound and David Jones as one of those poets 'in whom scholarship is an extension of intuitive knowledge' rather than something displayed in exercises in 'the gentle art of saying nothing elegantly or evading the here-and-now'. With astonishing attentiveness and verve, *Gods with Stainless Ears* records how the Second World War 'changes [the] contour' of the 'blue rinsing bay' of the estuary, but the poem also conveys a deep sense of history that intermittently reveals and conceals itself in the fluctuating tidescape of Roberts's Carmarthenshire home. This sense of history is underpinned by references to the 'Four Ancient Books of Wales', the medieval manuscripts known as *The Black Book of Carmarthen*, *The Book of Taliesin*, *The Book of Aneirin* and *The Red Book of Hergest*.

As part of her research, Roberts made frequent visits to the Carmarthen County Library, and occasionally to the National Library of Wales in Aberystwyth, as well as institutions in London. She was also regularly in correspondence with librarians and booksellers on the trail of what she needed, even swapping books by post with fellow poet and late modernist David Jones. A sense of her reading life, and her devotion to it, weaves its way through the intertexts and the footnotes of her long poem. But lines from the medieval Welsh elegy *Y Gododdin* (a lament for the fallen soldiers of the Battle of Catraeth around the year 600) are as likely to be spoken by a local lad in the pub as any bard or scholar.

Taking a radical position that reflected her desire to see culture from high art to traditional crafts like coracle making preserved, Roberts suggested to the writer and critic Robert Graves that 'authentic documents should be photographed & printed off, & be available to every person interested in studying them. To have only the rare document say in the [British Museum], fails in my opinion when those living outside the area cannot see it.' In the small Welsh village of Llanybri, where she spent the years of the war, and later as a single mother living a more precarious life in a caravan in Laugharne, Roberts felt this estrangement from culture keenly.

I'm sure that Roberts would have been pleased to see how digitisation projects have made hundreds of manuscripts and books more widely accessible (although the recent data hack at the British Library in 2023, and the subsequent loss of access to digitised manuscripts there, suggests that this access is still fragile and contingent). Despite digitisation, access remains deeply hierarchical: even if we set aside the question of who might feel they have the cultural capital in the first place to make a request, a letter of recommendation could be required to get access beyond the zoomable pixels of a screen, while other digitised resources are locked behind private portals. Anyone who has ever applied for a Reader's Card at the British Library will no doubt have seen countless others being turned away for not quite having their documents in order.

More than anything, Roberts's writing is testament to other ways of knowing and perceiving the world that should be valued alongside scholarship. These alternative ways of knowing find expression in an intimate attention to, and observation of, local environments: its flora and fauna, the habits of light, and mutable soundscapes. We might think of the lists Roberts kept in her diary of the flowers she had encountered in hedgerows and laneways along the coast, or the two baskets of stones and quartz pebbles she had collected from Cwmcelyn Bay and kept in her loft (as she confessed in a letter to the poet Alun Lewis), hoping that one day the Camarthen Museum might take them into their keeping. The quartz pebbles make an appearance in Roberts's tender 'Poem from Llanybri'; the poem is addressed to Lewis, but it also represents something of a love poem for a community she was trying to write her way into. In a revealing note from her diary in 1939, Roberts compared the 'intricate inner rhymes and alliteration' of the Welsh Englyn to Llanybri and by extension to the quartz pebbles she found on the beach: 'The poetic form itself like the village, like a piece of quartz'. How much of what is essential to a place might be contained in a single pebble? What might we come to know by tuning our attention to the materiality, form and tactility of a rock? Such questions extend beyond the pebbles in the basket in the loft, to the knowledge that might be gained from material and sensorial encounters of all kinds.

Following the trail of Lynette Roberts back to the Art Library has given me an excuse to luxuriate in the vegetal furls and arches of the *Camaldolese Gradual/Grail*'s illuminated initials, to consider the manuscript's strange iconography, to touch the hair side of the parchment and catch the whiff of this book's haunted animal smell, to move away from the screen and comprehend how the scale and physicality of a book might also speak to its ritual and symbolic purpose. When I set out for London, I didn't know exactly what I hoped to get from my appointment with this medieval manuscript, but I understand better now the fierceness of Roberts's assertion of her right to respond intellectually and creatively to the *Camaldolese Gradual/Grail*, and her insistence on the time she had spent in the manuscript's presence. I can't help but wonder too, if there was any trace of Roberts's encounter with this fourteenth-century Italian manuscript in the dust catalogued in 2009, which I have inadvertently given so much attention to on my visit; this dust that records an extended, decaying history of prohibition and access to this magnificent object.

Wheatfields with Reaper

JOE WINTER

Thatched Cottages

Merely an ordinary
tumbledown story
of folk and their tall tales.

Blossoming Chestnut Trees

A great chandelier
of candles. Will the gossiping
ladies fall quiet at the light?

The House of Père Pilon

The house is hidden
by a tree which commands
the sky as a halo.

Blossoming Chestnut Branches

Blind bankrupts of storm –
a white-flowered branch
and a pink-flowered spray, still in business.

View of Auvers-sur-Oise (i)

A falling-in-place:
wheat, trees, rooves,
and the steam of a train passing by.

View of Auvers-sur-Oise (ii)

Out there, a neat bareness
of hill and village.
Up close, a writhing hedge-scramble.

Doctor Gachet's Garden

A tree-beast reared up –
an armed wave of growth
fierce as the sun, sharp as scissors.

Farmhouse

Roofed against uncertainty,
nothing is on easier terms
with the sky, than the daily chore.

Farmhouses in Auvers-sur-Oise

In the fixity of the moment,
the other side of the maelstrom,
a benign outpost of Time.

Marguerite Gachet in the Garden

Marguerite, where you walk
a rich land-plot defers –
to usher you on, in abundance.

Roses and Turban Buttercups

How can the unmindful be
companions, aunts, sisters?
They know more than we think.

Absinthe Glass with Wild Flowers

A chiselled face pauses
in a tangle of reflections,
observations, and red and white memories.

Doctor Paul Gachet

Ah my friend,
my friend the good doctor,
a heal-all – if listening could heal!

The Church at Auvers-sur-Oise

The wayward lines
of life meet at one –
all tracks and all trails, all directions.

Blossoming Acacia

Merely a branch
of who knows what
instance and circumstance.

Glass with Carnations

Crammed, free and speaking –
the exuberant breath
of a fortunate storehouse.

Bouquet of Flowers in a Vase

What words and what laughter,
what a shindig! – or merely
the loveliest greeting.

Green Wheatfields

To re-imagine the Earth,
to make new dips in the sky,
this is the art of the wind.

Vineyards at Auvers-sur-Oise

A swirl of vine-tangle –
a dash of poppy and red-roof –
in the depth of a village. Wine.

Poppy Field

The sky mirrors in blue
the voluble excitement
of a field in red.

Wheatfield with Cornflowers

Give me a flower
to take with me when I go...
the blue weeds in wheatfields.

Vase with Red Poppies, Cornflowers and Daisies

So many faces
upturned to the light
out of an earthen urn.

Les Vessenots in Auvers-sur-Oise

A way to peace:
to return to a village hamlet
as in a dream.

Daubigny's Garden

The quietest action
a life takes can be
to set foot on grass.

Ears of Wheat

At ground level only,
the story behind a tumultuous
spike-rustle.

Vase with Wild Flowers

Flinging stems, lunging leaves –
a glowing ragbag of faces
surprised by life.

White House at Night with Star

In the eye of night
a stillness... a tableau
of comings and goings.

Bank of the Oise at Auvers

Trim boats, a boat-owner,
two ladies... and a louche
unmannerly foliage.

Landscape at Twilight

What dark freight of night
arrives at the door
of the dusk hour.

Adeline Ravoux

She is who she is.
An irreducible soul,
an innkeeper's daughter.

Marguerite Gachet at the Piano

As you play, Marguerite
a waterfall idles
of notes, and your dress, and the rich day.

Two Girls

Strange...
these two imps, well equipped
to meet the dark world with a flower.

Child with Orange

Nothing gets better than this –
an orange, of all things! –
and somebody nearby to peel it.

Young Man with Cornflower

I had to paint it:
the cornflower, the green eyes,
and the flame of his flaxen hair.

Wheatfield with Reaper

The sun's touch is on the field.
Stooks stand, a man pauses:
they, he are one.

Field with Haystacks

They are frailer than they look,
the contours of things.
Haystacks, above all, come apart.

Rain at Auvers

Village, fields, trees,
a free estate thirsting
to be over-ruled in the rain.

Cottages in Chaponval

Given to nightmare,
the sleepy rooves avalanche down,
offering safety.

Wheatfield with Crows

A murder-posse of dark wings –
smoke from a field
in a torrent of unseen flame.

Tree Roots

Digging into the open –
it is there, a wild medley
yielded of earth. There and gone.

My 1950s

MARJORIE PERLOFF

My friend Anita Abbott and I, both in our early nineties, were reminiscing about the Old Days. 'The fifties,' she suddenly said with total conviction, 'was the best decade of my life.' I was startled. 'What about the treatment of Blacks', I asked. Or of gays, the fifties being, as I recall it, a horribly homophobic decade, when those even faintly suspect of being gay couldn't get job clearances. 'But most people were much happier then', she insisted. 'And we had so much fun.'

Perhaps hers was just a reaction to having been young and hence happier in her twenties. But I must confess I feel the same way. For me, the 1950s was somehow a golden age. Why? In *The Vienna Paradox* (2004), I wrote about my childhood years, first in Vienna and then as a refugee from Hitler in the United States. The paradox of the book's title refers to the contradiction between Viennese high culture – *Bildung* – as a form of religion versus the democracy of the United States, which functioned as a kind of alternative to it. At the turn of the twenty-first century, when I wrote *The Vienna Paradox*, I was probably much more positive about our democracy than I am today, and yet I still look back fondly on the Eisenhower years.

What was coming of age in the fifties really like? No story is more repeatedly misconstrued, whether in the movies, in novels, or in most historical accounts of the period. Films like *Far from Heaven* (2002) present the women of the 1950s as so many neurotic, pill popping ladies in high heels, shirtwaist dresses, and lots of red lipstick. These housewives, as they were known, are kept busy taking care of their children, but they never seem to play with them or to do anything with them. The husbands are even worse: arriving home from work exhausted and in need of the Big Drink, they plunk their children in front of the TV, happy to ignore them the rest of the evening. Everyone *has* children but who can stand being around them? Not in the world of John Updike or John Cheever.

Eventually in the narrative, a series of affairs and probably divorce as in *Mad Men*, which is the epitome of the fifties' suburban idyll gone sour. And yet the actual life of the 1950s was rather different! AT LEAST MY LIFE. Consider, for starters, the way social institutions worked in those days.

Marriage

I graduated from Barnard College in June 1953 and got married on July 31 of that year: I was twenty-one. Such early marriage was the norm in the postwar era. Why?

Surely it was not that people fell in love more readily in those days. But it was not yet the custom to rent one's own apartment and live on one's own; I for one would have been frightened to pursue the single life. Roommates were of course an option but made privacy impossible. Still, living 'at home' with one's parents? Surely not! Therefore, 'nice girls' (mostly still virgins) much preferred the prospects of early marriage, which meant having a man to support you. It seemed like the best solution. And with the G.I. Bill making college possible for millions of young men (although, strictly speaking, only white young men), marriage seemed to be the logical next step.

In the spring of '53, in any case, most conversations at the Robin Dell café on Broadway just south of Barnard College were about china and silver patterns, bridesmaids, and such. One would never know we were attending an institution of higher learning! Somehow everyone was 'pairing off', including myself.

I had transferred to Barnard precisely in the hope of meeting someone, although I would not have admitted this to anyone. At Oberlin, I knew all the eligible men and felt that there was no one for me. And I had taken all the most desirable courses like 'The Four Theatres' with the glamorous Professor Centeno, who related all theatrical modes to the varying conceptions of character of the three great Classical playwrights: Aeschylus, Sophocles and Euripides. That summer, I had a boyfriend named Rudy Boschwitz, who was also a refugee and was a law student at NYU. I was quite keen on Rudy until he told me he planned to move to Minnesota after graduation and open a lumber mill with his brother. Minnesota??? Lumber mill??? I knew that would never be the life for me. (Later, incidentally, Rudy became a Republican Senator from Minnesota.)

So that was the end of Rudy. I applied to Barnard and was accepted but I had no idea what Barnard would be like. At Oberlin, I had taken challenging courses like a year of Romantic poets, and a year of Elizabethan/Jacobean drama, but I had not taken the 'basics' – Chaucer, Milton, eighteenth century – so I had to take all three in my first semester. Even worse, I had to take math in my senior year as well as gym, which included miniature golf at the Riverside Church. I had been accepted for grad school in English at Columbia, but the new boring classes made me think that graduate school was not for me – at least not yet! Math, incidentally, was a hardship, because I never did understand why dividing a number by zero didn't simply yield zero?!

During the Christmas holidays, I was invited to a party by one Suzi Rosenthal whom I barely knew. I recall that later that evening I had a date with my brother's Reed College friend Eli Bergman. But I was sorry to leave the party because I had met this very attractive and sweet Southern gentleman-physician named Joseph Perloff. He wore a gray-blue wool suit I loved and a blue tie. Throughout *Tosca* (I am not a great opera fan), I thought about Joseph. (I did not like the name Joe.) That's how it began and by April, when I visited New Orleans, his hometown, we were engaged.

What a boring bourgeois story, yes? Could anything be more routine, triter? And yet consider the interesting wrinkles soon to manifest themselves in the grey blue suit. My arrival at New Orleans airport for example. I had never been to the South. In 1953 there were still signs everywhere, like 'For Colored Only' or its antitheses on streetcars 'Colored in rear of car only'. There were swimming pool signs like 'White Only' and so on. As a New Yorker, I had never seen such a thing and I found it very oppressive. I felt I could never live in such a place.

And then there was the family. All white, this time, all Jewish, but... Joe's father was a short little man with a huge bulging stomach and friendly but very homely face. He never stopped talking but I couldn't figure out what about – diamonds he had bargained for, his real estate businesses, and J.K. his very own 'boychik'. Rose, Joe's mother, was much taller than he was and more normal. But then there were all the aunts and uncles. Joe had three uncles, two of whom would never marry – Morris, Dave and Max. And there were similarly three aunts, Rae, Mimi and Sarah. Sarah was mentally impaired and sat in her bed all day sorting socks and doing other useful activities; Mimi was her caretaker. Rae had finally married and her husband Morris Warnick of course moved in with her and became part of the family. Only Max who had recently married Thelma, had moved out. But then Thelma was not Jewish so she didn't really count.

Including Joe's sister Shirley, who was my age and became a good friend, there were thus ten adults living at Number 5 Richmond Place in uptown New Orleans, plus the servants who were there every day: Augustine the cook, her husband Sergeant – a general factotum – and Lillian who did the laundry and upstairs cleaning. Needless to say, I had never met such a family before. Everyone ate when he or she felt like it; they would grab a plate and fill it with turkey, stuffing etc. Everyone was always kissing and hugging me which was not my style and they were always, in the heyday of TV, watching the Jack Benny show or Sid Caesar.

Could I really marry into such a family? My mother decided to go down on a visit so as to learn what the Perloff-Cohens were really like. She quite simply invited herself, which must've seemed quite odd to the New Orleans family, but of course they said yes and were extremely hospitable. She came home with a good report – that although Joe's family were wholly alien, they were good-hearted, decent people, who would treat me well. Meanwhile Joe was pronounced nearly perfect, what with his excellent manners and Southern charm. Indeed, grandmother Schuller declared that he looked like a handsome Italian, which was for her the ultimate compliment.

I myself worried secretly that Joe was not intellectual enough, that he had not read enough great books. This was to change very rapidly when we went on our honeymoon at St. Mary's Glacier Lake Lodge in Colorado, and he read and adored *War and Peace*. I also admired him for having been in the navy – I loved the pictures in uniform – and for knowing how to ride so well. He was wonderfully athletic, whereas I trudged up the glacier behind the hotel in my saddle shoes, smoking a cigarette and complaining of the cold. Joseph and I were so different, but Joe loved the idea of an educated European wife and so it all balanced out, without any of the artificial notion of common interests that dominates the dating scene today. Somehow, our marriages worked because we wanted them to work.

Work

A standard myth about the 1950s is that women did not work, that we were all homemakers. The actual situation was much more complicated. As college graduates, of course we planned to work, at least until we had children, which was usually three to four years or so. In my own case, we also needed the money, since Joe was doing another year of residency at Mt Sinai Hospital, and was paid almost nothing.

For what sort of job did an English major qualify? Publishing (the favourite), advertising, non-profit foundations, secretarial, receptionist, 'research'. Obviously, these jobs did not amount to much, my weak point being the artwork required in advertising, where I had neither the skills nor the imagination to proceed. My first job, in any case, was at the Bettmann Archive on 57th St – a wonderful location for lunch dates, what with all the art galleries and boutiques around. Old Dr Otto Bettmann, a German refugee, had assembled a picture archive of vast dimensions. He was alone in the office. Someone might call and want a nineteenth-century image of The Old Woman Who Lived in a Shoe. I would search the archive and find the best sample. I believe the pay was $40 per week.

It didn't take me more than a week to discover that this job was deadly dull. Moreover, Dr B. watched over me like a policeman: five minutes late after lunch meant a very dirty look. *Wissenschaft?*

Not really. So within six weeks, I quit.

My next job was as a 'title writer' for MGM. I followed up on an ad in the *New York Times* for a 'title writer trainee'. MGM wanted someone who was PBK (Phi Beta Kappa) and knew two foreign languages. Not that we ever used these languages. Title writing is basically condensation: since we don't read as quickly as we hear the words on film, cutting is essential. But the real task is the writing of 'alts', short for alternate lines. In *The Long, Long Trailer,* Lucille Ball tells Desi Arnaz, 'You turn left right here'. Of course the car swerves to the right. Get it? Or again, in *Kiss Me Kate,* Petruchio sings, 'If the wife has a bag of gold, / Do I care if the bag be old?' How to write a sentence in which the American slang 'old bag' comes across in, say, Italian or Arabic? A good alt anyone? The translators merely followed our texts: they did not see the films.

I spent many hours and smoked countless cigarettes playing the alt-pun game. It was especially hard in the case of Pete Smiths. No one knows Pete Smiths anymore: those horrible little shorts where the first guy drops all the eggs on the floor and the second one tries to pick them up. One time, I watched six Pete Smiths in a row and started to cry. My boss Bernie Doret couldn't imagine what was wrong. Why in the hell was I *crying*? 'Don't you understand?', I tried to explain, 'how stupid and meaningless this all is? It has no point. No one wants to see these films', and so on. Bernie disagreed. It was his view that the movies just gave people what they wanted. People loved these Pete Smiths. I decided then and there, I must do something 'meaningful' with my life, for example, go to graduate school. Even if the professors and classmates were going to be dull, at least the material would be inherently interesting.

I have never changed my mind about this simple idea. The literature itself, whether Thomas Browne's *Religio Medici* or Oscar Wilde's *De Profundis* – the essays, poems, plays – was always interesting. No more Long Long Trailers or images of Rosmarie in her raccoon hat! Joe had won a Fulbright scholarship to the National Heart Hospital in London and so before long we set off for what was my first trip to Europe – a truly wonderful year of travel and museum going. In London, moreover, I made the acquaintance of my mother's sister Hilde, an art historian married to fellow art historian Otto Kurz, who wrote the definitive book on fakes. The Kurzes, including bratty daughter Erica, then fourteen, immediately detected that Joe and I did not realize that the Leonardo *Madonna of the Rocks* in the National Gallery was a fake: the real one was in the Louvre whereas this one, as Erica proudly informed us, was only by Bernadino Luini.

In 1954, London was still in ruins: I remember especially the stones around Saint Paul's – a poignant sight. But in those days, you could drive down to Trafalgar Square or Kensington High Street and park anywhere. Few people owned cars, and the streets were still fairly empty. Supermarkets were not yet common; one shopped in a dozen little stores: the greengrocer, the stationer, the butcher, the baker. For me it was a real novelty and since I could not obtain green papers, I spent many hours and days reading. All of Proust, for instance, so that one time I was so absorbed I swallowed a plum pit. I read Mauriac and Malraux, Goethe's *Italienische Reise* and Thomas Mann's *Magic Mountain.* And of course art books like Bernard Berenson's *Italian Renaissance Painters,* in preparation for the big continental trip planned for the winter.

On that trip, we visited Vienna for a few days. What a disappointment! The Vienna of the fifties was still *Third Man* country: gloomy, dark, shabby and slightly sinister. Only old people in the streets and cafés. The beautiful buildings on the Ringstrasse mostly in ruins. People eyeing one another suspiciously. The concierges were consistently unfriendly. We couldn't wait to leave on the night train to Venice. And yet the recreation of the beautiful baroque Vienna of the eighteenth century was just around the corner. Change comes so quickly in our time.

But we weren't there to see it because in the summer of 1955 we moved to Washington where Joe had a cardiology fellowship at Georgetown, and I attended graduate school at Catholic University. And thereby hangs a complicated tale.

It always astonishes me how powerful custom is. Does no one strike out on their own? In the fifties, the term 'single mother' was barely known: I don't believe I knew a single one, except for my dear fellow refugee friend Corinna Metcalf, who had lived in Paris on her own and was bringing up Alexander quite without the help of his father, the painter Jimmy Metcalf. Today, when every would-be Congressman brags about his single mother and what she did for him, this may seem an odd state of affairs, but there it is. In my day, husbands were *de rigueur* – points on a map, so to speak, that determined where the couple in question lived, what jobs they held, and so on. The role of husbands was to make enough money to buy a house, but in the meantime, they oversaw the search for apartments – primarily in new buildings, with largish living rooms, smallish dining areas, kitchens and bathroom with latest equipment, and two bedrooms.

Ours, in Washington, D.C., which we rented after we returned from our year in England, was in a new building called the Phylmar Plaza, in a corner of the Glover Park neighbourhood surrounded by parkland and parking lot – no garages yet then. The rent was $150 per month (roughly $1,700 today). It was less than a ten-minute drive to Georgetown Hospital where Joe was doing a residency in cardiology. The Phylmar Plaza is still there, looking exactly as it did in 1956.

Was the Phylmar Plaza in any way distinctive? Not at all, but it had an elevator, the woods of Glover Park behind it, and you could usually park in front. Convenience was very important in those days.

Living in Washington

But why Washington to begin with? I said earlier that I couldn't imagine living in New Orleans. By the same token, Joe did not want to live in New York. Too expensive for a physician who wants to open a practice (which Joe thought at the time he would do). The people were too rude! No one gave their seats in the subway to old ladies! You couldn't park your car: we often double-parked our little green Oldsmobile all night and, in the morning, it was likely to have new dents and scratches.

At the same time, our city had to be cosmopolitan and have cultural attractions! Joe's best friend, Billy Kohlmann, who, on the plane to Paris in the early fifties was stricken with polio and spent months in an iron lung, was in Washington, working for the State Department, or so he said – it was really the CIA. Billy had a circle of very interesting friends from the Agency. In those days, grad students who had M.A. degrees but were reluctant to go on to a PhD often worked for the government or for the foreign service for a few years. Agencies like the AID, the USIS, and of course the State Department itself were popular, operating on a largely nine-to-five basis so that there was plenty of time for cocktail parties and dinners at local restaurants. Everyone had parties on weekends or went to them, and there would be much gossip about Sargent Shriver's latest speech or the chaotic activities at Robert Kennedy's Hickory Hill.

The Washington of those years was a small town. There was not yet a subway but anyone that one was likely to know lived in the north west in easy driving distance of one another. When our children were small, we would put them in the car in what were then standard little car seats (not the monsters of today) and have art/poetry visits – little salons where discussion of books and artworks was central. One key hostess was Meryle Secrest, who is still publishing biographies, the latest being of Princess Margaret Rose and foetal alcohol syndrome.

Meryle was an Englishwoman from Bath. As was customary then, she did not attend university but became a journalist. In Washington, she got her start by writing social columns – very boring to do she said – and then her first biography of Romaine Brooks, the great lesbian French salonnière and friend of Gertrude Stein. Then came Bernard Berenson, Frank Lloyd Wright – the list goes on and on.

Many interesting and talented women in our little kiddie group but my personal favourite and closest friend was an artist named Carrie Westervelt. Carrie was astonishing. She was beautiful, very funny, and aside from painting in the tradition of Kenneth Noland and Ellsworth Kelly, her teachers at American University, she could recite, over lunch at Martin's in Georgetown, all of Donne's 'Canonization' or Wordworth's 'Resolution and Independence'.

University

Whatever Washington is or isn't, it is not a university town. In 1955, the University of Maryland suffered a major football scandal and didn't offer a PhD in English. No PhDs in the Humanities were offered at George Washington, American University, Georgetown, or Howard either. When I consulted my favourite Oberlin professor, F.X. Roellinger, where I might go, he suggested Catholic University, a place that had never crossed my mind since it was the Pontifical University and most of its faculty and students were clergy. For someone Jewish who had gone to two protestant liberal arts colleges – Oberlin and Barnard – Catholic University was quite a culture shock. The first course I signed up for was English Renaissance literature, taught by the department Chair Kirby Neill. We called him Kirby Nihil because his mind seemed so deliciously empty. Studying the Renaissance sonnet, the classification system was by number: is this sonnet by Sidney a 12+2 or 10+4 or 8+6? Where, in other words, is the turn or volta? In Shakespeare, what with the closing couplet, it is usually 12+2, but not necessarily, for the meaning structure can override the sound structure.

Meanwhile, we were busy reading Hiram Haydn's *Counterrenaissance* and C.S. Lewis's *The Literature of the Sixteenth Century in England.* From these two books, especially the Lewis, I learned that the Renaissance had definitely been a Bad Thing, inimical to Christian humanism. But wait a minute: hadn't our Oberlin professors taught us that everything good began with the Renaissance, as the very notion of rebirth made clear? So how could the word have these negative implications?

In class I sat next to Father Jordan who was always complimenting me on my sweaters. How to react to that mode of behaviour?? And in Craig LaDrière's theory class, we were learning that the highest faculty – the faculty that only the angels have – was called the *vis cogitativa.* Hmmm – I had never heard of that one at Oberlin. Soon I was having discussions about the meaning of *grace* in *Measure for Measure* and coming to terms with *mimesis vs diegesis* in Aristotle. It was all very challenging and new. And not without its problems.

I signed up for Goethe taught by a mournful priest. The only other student in this seminar was a young man from Gallaudet, Washington's well-known college for the hearing impaired. This student leaned over my shoulder and copied my notes: what else could he do? But I stopped writing anything because the priest wasn't saying anything. Occasionally I would write down, 'Sorry, he isn't saying anything worth taking down'. This meant that when I dropped the course a week or two later, my new friend had to drop it too.

And then there was French Romanticism taught by a recent convert from Judaism to Catholicism, Helmut Hatzfeld, who was quite well known at the time for his studies in stylistics. Hatzfeld's main goal was to distinguish between the truly religious poets (e.g. Châteaubriand) and those capable of no more than *religiosity* like Dostoyevsky. I was in the doghouse from the beginning because I chose Alfred de Musset as my special author and was evidently not critical enough of the great love affair with George Sand. In other words, Hatzfeld did not like my tone: he found it frivolous; I seemed to take the 'tragedy' too lightly. 'Do you find this amusing, Mrs. Perloff?', he asked me after my presentation. The fact is that I probably did! It was so absurdly romantic! But I was not surprised when I got a B+ in French Romanticism.

Graduate School was so different in those days. There were no graduate fellowships: rather one paid tuition which I recall amounted to about $600 in 1955–6. Being accepted at Catholic University was not a problem; if you could pay the tuition, you got in. And I planned to do my MA degree in two semesters and be done by June 1956. It was especially important to carry out this plan, because by January I found out I was pregnant – again, according to plan. Nancy was born on 1 September 1956.

Mine, I later found out, was quite a normal way of doing things in the fifties. Since fees were low one could take one's time writing one's MA thesis: mine was on privileged moments in Proust and Virginia Woolf – a topic that no longer especially interests me since it was purely thematic. Those PM's or 'moments of being' were not hard to find, especially not in *Mrs. Dalloway* or of course in Proust's 'Combray'. Most afternoons, I sat in the library making my way through my very long novels with relative ease. Much more interesting to me was LaDrière's course on sound and meaning, and poetry began to occupy me more than did fiction. Wasn't poetry, after all, the heart of literature? And wasn't it quite exciting that Ezra Pound was in residence at Saint Elizabeth's, where LaDrière and Giovannini were regular visitors and personal friends of the poet?

My friend Elizabeth Hartley, a shy and beautiful girl, arranged to go visit Pound one day. She returned horribly disillusioned. Evidently Pound, who was wearing Bermuda shorts, did nothing but recite favourable reviews of his poetry from the Italian newspapers. His sometime mistress Sheri Martinelli was there, stroking the great man's ego. And the company included those charming fascists John Kasper and Eustace Mullins.[1] Elizabeth never went back, indeed never wanted to hear Pound's name again. As for me, Pound was still a remote quantity: my first true love among modernist poets being W.B. Yeats, who was no doubt an odd choice for a Jewish girl from Vienna. Not Greek but Irish mythology and Gaelic folklore, not secular humanism but faith in the occult, in mysticism, and Irish versus English politics. Yeats was to serve as an Irish Senator in his later days; his book *A Vision* (1926) was an elaborate cosmology that measured the phases of life by the twenty-eight phases the moon passed through in its journey from dark through full (phase fifteen) and back again. Maud Gonne, with whom Yeats was in love for most of his life, may have been a great beauty; she was also, in later life, a proto-Nazi, whose 'revolutionary' politics were hugely questionable. 'Where had her sweetness gone?' Yeats asked in 'Quarrel in Old Age' and could only respond with the words, 'I had forgiven enough / who had forgiven old age'.

When it came to his beloved women, Yeats was in fact not very forgiving. Eva Gore-Booth and Con Markiewicz, the two Lissadell beauties, had destroyed their charm by letting their voices 'grow shrill' with conspiracy plots and political lust. As for his male friends like Patrick Pearse, Thomas MacDonagh, the big question remains what good their revolutionary activity did? 'Oh when may it suffice?' And there is no easy answer.

'Easter 1916' is surely one of the great political poems in the English language. But my love of Yeats also depended on sound. The trimeter of 'Easter 1916', or the mimesis of sounds as in

/ / / || / /
Speech after long silence: it is right.

where the sound reacts precisely to what is happening: in this case the burst of speech after silence with the caesura as marker and then the sign of approval. Five major stresses, but in a wholly irregular sound structure. Or again take the famous 'Sailing to Byzantium':

/ / / / || /
That is no country for old men. The young
/ / / | / /
In one another's arms, birds in the trees,
/ / / || / /
– Those dying generations – at their song,
/ / / / /
The salmon-falls, the mackerel-crowded seas,

/ /\ / / /\ /
Fish, flesh, or fowl, commend all summer long
/ / / / /
Whatever is begotten, born, and dies.
/ / / / /
Caught in that sensual music all neglect
/ / / / /
Monuments of unageing intellect.

I remember the *frisson* of reading that opening line – which was to become the title of Cormac McCarthy's popular novel and film – for the first time in 1956, marvelling at the seemingly casual and conversational use of the demonstrative pronoun 'that', with its dismissal of Ireland, evidently the country of the old, in contrast to the young, introduced at the end of the run over line. The stanza is *ottava rima* (abababcc, eight lines of iambic pentameter) which in Yeats's case is wilfully irregular, 'young'

1 John Kasper (1929–1998), politician, segregationist and Ku Klux Klan member. Eustace Mullins (1923–2010), antisemitic conspiracy theorist, Holocaust denier and white supremacist. Both men considered themselves disciples of Pound.

and 'song' constituting only an approximate rhyme as does 'dies' in the 'trees', 'seas', 'dies' sequence. Mortality – those dying generations – is stressed throughout: that which lives and flourishes – 'the young in one another's arms', 'the salmon-falls, the mackerel crowded seas' is also doomed to death. 'Sailing to Byzantium' is to leave living behind for the sake of art, immortality, permanence, 'monuments of unageing intellect'.

Why was I so captivated by the sounds of poetry that I decided to change my major field of study? Perhaps a new conviction that poetry has its own language and wastes no words, as when Eliot composes the couplet:

> Of restless nights in one-night cheap hotels
> And sawdust restaurants with oyster-shells –

A couplet remarkably memorable like the last line of 'Prufrock', 'Till human voices wake us, and we drown'. A kind of magical mathematics so that poetry can be 'News that stays news', in Ezra Pound's words.

I was, in any case, enjoying myself in graduate school and I had also made quite a few friends, a number of whom were Black, since Howard University did not at that time give a PhD and sent its students to Catholic University. One of them was Eleanor Traylor, who was to become a star of the Howard faculty.

Flamboyant and funny, Eleanor always referred to her dissertation as a paper. It was on John Donne: there was as yet no real emphasis on African-American studies. I remember Eleanor giving our modern novel professor James Hafley a hard time over Faulkner's *The Sound and the Fury,* when we came to the words in the Appendix. 'Dilsey. They endured'. 'Dr. Hafley,' she insisted, 'They *endured?* Is that all?'

This work remains unfinished, as Marjorie Perloff died on 24 March 2024.
It has been lightly edited by Kit Kumiko Toda, John Solt and Charles Bernstein.

Eclipse

STEPHANIE BURT

Don't borrow trouble,
says the sun,
then ducks out of sight.

Somebody holds up a sheet of synthetic
mica. A pinhole; a needle
jammed through blank cardboard.

All our own fires
too, will someday
go out. We stand

for an hour with sorrow
over our covered
eyes, while the moon's

body double
pretends she can protect us
with her shadow, as if

whatever we had to afford
to lead a happy life had
become too much

for us to swallow, as if
we too had to keep
within its numbing

penumbra, away
from dangers too
old to remember,

as if the last logs had
cooled from gold to
maroon: we watch our

rustic-minded sister and
father sweep the dusty
lintels, then clean

our faces and head right off
to bed, too young
to see the last few embers.

The Accidental Curator

RICHARD PRICE

1.
Butterfly Colony

It's my last day in the office at the British Library, a dark November day in 2024. The white-yellow lighting feels especially bright. I'm 'The Head of Contemporary British Collections' for another fifteen minutes. Though I'm on my own I feel self-conscious, as if I am being watched. I know every little task I've done today, every encounter, has been my last here.

It is odd to sign off payments of tens of thousands of pounds knowing they are both routine and final acts. A bill for a sound archive contract comes in on my laptop. A few checks, a few clicks on the finance system, and it's done. I assign another part of the budget, this time for an oral history project. Unusually it's about the Library itself. We've been talking about it on and off for months. It's the next phase of a long-going institutional memory project that stretches back many years. Even so it is always stop-start to fund. In this iteration we are making sure we hear the experience of workers in the lower ranks, not just the high-ups. Click, done.

I'll tell my own story in writing.

In the very last minutes of the job there's a super-sensitivity in the air – it's like the feeling you have as you go into an interview and suddenly you're aware of all your thoughts and none, how you will never be able to answer the simplest question; you're not sure you'll be able to confirm your name. But you do of course and much more. After all, just such an interrogation started your career in the first place. It was a second ago, if thirty-six years count as a second.

Sounds are heightened. I can hear a couple of teaching colleagues in the Learning department across from me conferring quietly about their latest project to inspire young people. I can hear the waves of the photocopier round the corner as it builds layer on paper layer, handouts perhaps for the children, or maybe a funding spreadsheet. It has been my good fortune in the last ten years to share this space with those dedicated to the young, helping them to love the archive, helping them to question everything about it, too.

My own team are here on this floor and in various other enclaves of expertise around the building: fifty or so library specialists who are experts on a vast range of manuscripts, printed books and digital publications, on newspapers and broadcast news, on web archiving, sound and film, and on audio engineering. I have to list them all to believe it all. Together we've been managing an annual budget of about £3.5m and I'm the sign-off merchant.

A butterfly colony of yellow and orange Post-it notes has established itself across my office wall, their bright colours all around. Visitors have told me how the scale and blend of these vivacious little oblongs of paper make the whole space look like an art installation. There are words and phrases on each, like 'Sport', 'Technological response', and 'User View?'.

Ten years ago I had been offered this space when it was a forgotten prop room for our exhibitions programme. For a while I lived with huge cut-outs of sinister figures from a Propaganda exhibition, but I was able to have them moved on in the end. Post-its' association with concept art seems about right to me, here in my office and in general. It's also in tune with my own quizzical experience of managerial life: sometimes amused, sometimes appalled, but usually trying to make a pretty pattern out of it all. I guess you could say the same for my take on poetry, too.

Now I'm all packed up and ready to go. At the office door I look back and see a wooden-handled paper-knife left on my desk. It has a Crown property imprint, a little Crown burnt into the wood. I feel for the tree. The knife is a relic of my time in the British Museum building in the 1990s. Chance had it I was one of the two last curators staffing the enquiry desk in the Round Reading Room before it was closed. I have used the knife many times since – sometimes with life-threatening enthusiasm – opening booksellers' catalogues on topics from local history to erotica to the history of science. Though I'm seen as a 'literary' curator, and poetry was part of my brief, too, there was an encyclopaedic breadth to the role, and I have missed it since middle management came a-calling.

If I had stayed as a junior curator, the paper-knife would still have been at rest: almost all the booksellers' catalogues we work with have long since gone online if they haven't closed. When a letter has come in, it has felt like a sacred rite to prise open the envelope and tease out the folded contents. Hand-writing is a personal whisper to an email's dead-pan announcements.

I leave the knife there.

I take one last glance at the remains of my old computer terminal, still disabled by the cyber-attack which hit us over a year ago. The hard disk is impounded somewhere else in the building, so it's just screen and keyboard. I've got so used to using my own laptop instead that what's left of my work PC has the aura now of an exhibit in an industrial heritage museum. The bits and bobs might as well be wringer and washboard from the shopfloor of a commercial laundry back in the day.

I cherish a proper letter but I am still mourning the digital loss. That loss is as much about idealism as risk of actual damage. Right from the start of my career I've had an active interest in the liberating potential of the electronic. So this feeling is not a Luddite gloat. It's a shocked elegy for the optimism of the early days of digital revolution. A career highpoint, for example, was pushing for a UK web archive and securing it in my team, decades ago: the sheer exuberance of underground information, of new networks, of new expression, just had to be captured. Though it was hard to do with the short-term cost-consciousness of a public body, embodied in its bureaucracy, we did more than make a start.

In fact we are told that the electronic collections in our care, archives so vast now they outnumber the Library's entire collection of printed books and manuscripts, are 'almost certainly' still intact. Noone likes 'almost certainly', but I trust that assessment: slowly we have been able to open up the first of the virtual collections and they've been fine. There is no reason to think unopened ones will be any different and we know that certain preservation protocols, which duplicated data for safety, were followed.

Yet the programs which are necessary to arrange and access our e-journals, our e-books, web-archives, our digital manuscripts, you name it, have all been 'scorched'. We will have to wait longer. It will still be months, perhaps years, before many of those digital objects will be available again. It's the thought that a library built expressly for the safeguarding and sharing of public knowledge should have been attacked so brutally, that the digital era so many of us had such hope for should turn out so unprotected and fragile – all this data, once targeted, so hard to recover – it's that thought which preoccupies me. I was always going to go now, when the sums of early retirement started to work in my favour – but I would never have thought I would be going at such a low point for the Library.

I shut the office door for the last time.

As I do so I'm stopped by something that catches my eye. It's a favourite inscription on a Post-it note, isolated from the others. I can't actually see the writing from here but I know what it says. Listen, Innovate, Share. I still believe in it.

I close the door gently and walk out of the building. 'Listen, Innovate, Share', I say quietly, out loud. Either I'm talking to myself or into one of those mobile phones you can't see.

2.
The News

Who can say why, if we have much choice at all, we choose one career over another? Who can say what truly underlies our enthusiasms and obsessions?

It's clear to me that information and song have been core to me from the earliest age. I suppose there is the ghost of a vocation in these interests but I don't like the thought of work being the answer to fascination, drive or joy.

Instead there's a personal algebra that I see as set aside from the realms of education and employment: Information + Song = Poetry. Either that equation has guided me through the years or I've interpreted everything that has happened through it. I did end up the head of a large national library department devoted to all three elements (and more), but that still seems accidental.

Work has obviously occupied most of my waking time, but I have written very little about it in the half century I've been writing. You could say the same for school. Perhaps it is because they have both been so dominant. It was hard keeping a sense of self while I was within their authority, and though 'resisting' is too strong a word for the mental protections anyone has to put in place under such conditions it's not too far off. Devoting yet more time to 'remembering' employment, now that I am finally free, is perverse, I know, but at least I have flung myself clear. I can look at the overall shape of whatever it was I have left.

And when I say 'information' I start much more sensually and personally than that dry word might imply. As a toddler I was in awe of the manifestations of news before I had any inkling of news's meaning: the huge folded newspaper, as if alive, flapping through the letterbox each morning, and my father eagerly fetching it if I hadn't already scampered ahead of him.

As for song, well the Beatles, weren't they four boys just like me and my three brothers? Their almost endlessly inventive melodies rang out on the click-clack tape player my eldest brother Tim shared with us.

'I wanna hold your hand!', 'Help!' – the Beatles seemed enthusiastic, playful, wise even. They used everyday phrases and applied a joyful torque of meaning that maybe the everyday didn't automatically have. Their projected personalities even sketched out a mythic pattern of life: amiable Ringo and his nursery rhymes for the first years of childhood, aggy John for the teenage years of question, precocious reflection and protest; and the comfort, pathos and sparkle of Paul for adult life. Finally, George's ascetism for the last days.

I have always liked the simplicity and fragility of a newspaper, so perfect in its first smooth folds, and, in contrast to its bluster of robust rhetoric, so quick to decay. I have the simple memory of seeing my father placing a page of broadsheet over the hearth to revive a stalled fire. We lived in a stylish brand-new bungalow on a private estate which had very recently been farmland – the buildings of one of the farms were still there and new homes would go up in the fields for many years – but it was not so modern as to lack a fireplace. A coal lorry duly delivered sacks of coal for our bunker and my father enjoyed the ritual of fire-making as much as I did.

By drawing in the room's air, a sheet of news would encourage a reluctant fire to stir. Soon there'd be a roar in the grate. For a few seconds the orange light would backlight the newspaper's paragraphs, a face here, a face there, and then a dark blister would appear and grow and pucker until leaves of bright flame took over and my father would let the fire consume what remained.

The papers had a special significance in the household because Tim was a paper boy. By the time I was seven or eight I was allowed to tag along with him on his round, becoming more and more fascinated with the rhythms of the news's dramatic content, the whole world patterned onto sheets of shared paper. I was fascinated by its silences, too: why did the topics of the stories seem so distant, a kind of art sufficient to itself, the way that a song in an unknown language becomes abstract, the repeated, delimited patterns the focus of attention?

Even now I can feel the weight of that dirty yellow canvas bag Tim used to carry on his round. He was in his early teens and I could barely lift that bag. He'd be up at half six to walk the mile to the newsagent to pick up the cargo and there'd be a couple more miles of the paper round itself. I'd only be allowed to go with him on a Saturday. Once underway he'd stop at the foot of a drive, hand me the paper, and I'd scurry up to the door. Because the bag was so heavy I wasn't allowed to carry it for him until half the round was complete. Then I was proud to. I had the same feeling a child might have when a grownup first hands them the lead of the family dog, 'Yes, you can walk her'.

The dirt of the ink of the newspapers rubbed off everywhere, on the bag, on your hands, and, something you'd notice in the mirror back home, somehow on your face, too. Words and even fragments of sentences got onto your skin, and I imagined the right word landing on the right part of your body, 'finger' on finger, 'nose' on nose, the creation of self-described humans. Years later I'd design a poetry workshop on that principle, inviting students to write a special type of haiku which would be tattooed onto the area of the body to which the poem itself alluded. I called these 'taku', merging content and form – they're collected in *Moon for Sale* (Carcanet, 2017).

I grew up in the dormitory settlements of Renfrewshire, villages west of Glasgow. We'd deliver *Glasgow Heralds,* one or two *Scotsman* (more of a local Edinburgh paper despite its title), and even an English broadsheet like the *Daily Telegraph*. The few *Telegraphs* went to some of the mansions up towards the golf course, the homes of the power class, they thought. The lurid reds of Scotland's leftish tabloid the *Daily Record* marked a paper my parents would never have let past the threshold, but it went to homes rich and poor. Moving to Scotland in the mid-sixties my mother and father had changed, I can only guess, from *Manchester Guardian* people to *Glasgow Herald* people, broadsheet liberals acclimatising.

My brother was a firebrand with a keen analytical sense of what he was pushing through people's letterboxes. He had been involved in various controversies at school and had, in my father's eyes, 'even fallen in with' working class boys from council homes. They lived on the other side of the village but we all mixed in the local school, bar the very wealthy. My mother welcomed one and all when Tim brought them home, as if raising four children of her own was merely training for more shenanigans when a band of little men came to call.

Tim would tell me how the press wasn't the whole world at all, how so many worthwhile stories would never make the page, and he wasn't just a talker. He organised all the newsagent lads in a paperboy strike. The first effect of this was that the shop owner had to deliver the papers himself. Tim's round was just one of several going out from the shop – another boy delivered our paper, for example – so this would have been a marathon task for the man.

Precisely where my parents heard 'the news' about the strike I don't know. Tim was a secretive person as far as authority was concerned, and I wonder if he even gave my parents advance warning. I like to think the first my parents heard of it was when the newsagent, let's call him Mr McRae, delivered our morning paper and rang our doorbell. I see the scene now:

Dad: 'Delivering your own papers today, McRae?'
Mr McRae: awkwardly, holding back: 'That's right, Mr Price'.
Dad: 'One of the lads not feeling well this morning?'
Mr McRae: handing Dad the *Herald*. 'Not exactly....'
Dad: [Eyebrows in a question mark]
Mr McRae: 'They're on strike!'
Dad: 'The cheeky...' Stops short of swearing. Thinks for a second. 'It'll be one boy egging them all on. You need to find the ringleader and get rid of him pronto!'
Mr McRae: 'I wanted to speak with you about that, Mr Price.'

In any case, my mother and father must have been torn between embarrassment, a kind of pride in Tim's leadership, and a concern for his mental health. My father would also have been exasperated with a son he had long struggled to see eye to eye with. There was also the odd fact that he himself had once led a successful schoolkid strike. He told me, years later, that this was during the War. Against the agreement, the farmer refused to pay his potato-picking gang, a cadre of older schoolchildren. The police had even got involved. 'Are you a Communist, son?' they asked, Communism being the era's version of Must Be Having Mental Issues. But collective action carried the day, even when the country was practically under martial law.

The 1970s were changed times and clearly my father had changed, too. In my parent's minds the mechanism of a collective strike was not evidence, in a system where individuals would otherwise be picked off one by one, of the necessity of forming defensive groups but of personal psychosis. Encouraged in that view by media narratives which personalised every motivation rather than imagined communities working together, they booked Tim in to see a child psychologist.

Why he wasn't summarily sacked I don't know. Perhaps it was just such a shock in this sleepy village that it took time for Mr McRae to know what to do. And soon enough Tim and the lads won, securing a wage increase for all. Of course it was not a story covered in the local news – or the national press, though I would have thought it warranted it.

The psychology sessions stopped.

The affair was a case study of one of those gaps in the news Tim knew all about. I suppose his radicalism – if it is radical to remember yourself, that you have worth and worth within a community – is the third influence he had on me beyond news and the lyric. I guess I'll have to adjust my arithmetic: information + song + *politics* = poetry.

Every poet has their own equation, of course. The maths is big enough. Later, under different conditions, I'll develop a completely different sum – painted + spoken – but it doesn't replace the first. Tim never renounced his instinctive socialism, though heaven knows there are times I've bitten my tongue.

3.
Just One Last Question

My first encounters with newspapers at the side of my brother widen and deepen into my teenage years. I take on an afternoon paper round myself, delivering the *Evening Times* around the village. There is one customer who leaves his door key on a string dangling through the letter box into his hall, a vestige of trust from an older world. I feel like a priest with confidences to keep.

Tim's at technical college now and in the evening we revise together at the kitchen table, a paper next to our jotters. It's the John Peel show on the radio. At times we drink pint glasses of black instant coffee to keep us up.

He's good at cryptic crosswords. I'm not but I have a posher vocab now and we defeat the puzzler together.

Tim: '*Rex's trawler forges fond days.* Seven letters. This has got to have something to do with kingfisher.'

Me: 'Halcyon?'

We finish our homework and watch *Newsnight* together in the front room. We stay up late if there's an election on.

At school I am one of only two boys to take Secretarial Studies, in my case so I can learn to touch-type, a serious advantage in the reporting life. On the first day I sit with my classmate Kevin but we are separated permanently for talking. We had been discussing what the lyrics to 'Come on Eileen' *really* mean. I am starting to write the words for songs myself, inspired by two sides of Sam Cooke, the politics of 'A change is gonna come', the sweetness of 'Wonderful World'.

I leave school at the age of sixteen, sitting a competitive entrance exam to take a one-year Diploma in Journalism at Napier College, Edinburgh. I do well there and I edit the class newspaper, my first experience of the magic of photo-litho printing. With its direction by computer control it feels a modern process, but later I find it's closely related to the making of images in biscuit tin production, from the nineteenth century. I continue to write poems and I make a little book of them, typed up directly onto pale blue paper and stapled together, *Peaches.* I pick up the class prize for exam results.

Traditionally my next step would have been to find a position as a cub reporter at a local newspaper, but I pause. I'm shy, and I'm still thirsty to read and think. As far as real work is concerned, like Melville's Bartleby, I'd rather not. I find a degree course that mixes information with literature, Librarianship and English Studies, and I take it, spending four years at Strathclyde University, Glasgow.

Then it really is time to work. I've put it off long enough. I've had temporary jobs of course, from picking raspberries on a local farm (my girlfriend was the farmer's daughter) to freelance gardening, from inputting barcode data in a university library to indexing the biography of the poet Hugh MacDiarmid. I have even worked in London before, as a student library assistant on summer placement at the Ministry of Agriculture in Whitehall.

Permanent jobs are not easy to find. I'm caught in the middle of a major restructuring of society, driven by England's South-East. Thatcher has been skimming the revenues from North Sea oil to de-industrialise the north of England, Wales and Scotland; breaking the power of trade unions to hyper-individualise what remains of the workplace; and removing rail and energy from public ownership. Her party have been using Scottish oil revenues to pay out huge sums in unemployment benefit: the totals are vast, the individual payments small. Her party have shifted the UK's 'growth' to the financial sector, centred on the global corporations of the City of London.

In short, the late 1980s are not a promising time in Scotland. I try to stay in the country at least. I had taken an extra course in statistics at university so I apply to the accountancy firm Arthur Andersen. They invite me in to their grand offices in George Square in Glasgow and so far so good until the very end.

'What are your hobbies, Mr Price? There are some great golf courses out where you live. Bridge of Weir, and Kilmacolm!'

'Poetry', I say. I see the temperature drop to freezing.

'Mainly', I add, but we both know where we are now.

Well, Arthur Andersen folded in the early 2000s after a management consultancy scandal. Perhaps they could have done with more wild-eyed poets on their staff, or even trustworthy accountants. I suspect though the problem was structural, and still is, given the number of corruption stories their surviving peers keep getting themselves caught up in. As I'd say later: 'The world warms, but the human temperature is cooler. / Greed looms out of scale, without watch or word.' ('Snailmail', collected in *Moon for Sale,* Carcanet, 2017).

The only other interview in Scotland I manage to secure is on Orkney, for the role of school librarian of Stromness Academy. My organisational skills aren't exactly demonstrated when I leave it too late and the plane from Inverness to Kirkwall is all booked up. The panel, to my chagrin, stay on an extra day to give me the benefit of the doubt.

They are much kinder on my poetry interests than Arthur Andersen. But I still don't get the job. Fair's fair, the idea that I could just walk into as complex a role as school librarian straight from university was sheer hubris.

I thank the foolish confidence of youth for the good fortune of it all, in fact. After the interview, more than suspecting I hadn't got the job, I visit the enigmatic site of the Rings of Brodgar, its tall stones still resonating abstraction and mystery after thousands of years. Then I go out to see the Neolithic homestead of Scara Brae. Its dwellings are hunkered down together. The site seems like a futuristic stand at an Ideal Homes Exhibition. I am not sure if I'm in the deep past or days soon to come. I look at those hearths and bed-boxes and wonder, where will I eventually settle?

When I return home there's a letter waiting with Civil Service branding on the envelope and maybe it contains the answer. The Civil Service Commission at that time act as a filter for applications to the British Library and I've applied there for a straightforward cataloguing job. I open it and find I've been invited to an interview, in Whitehall no less.

In a couple of weeks I bus down from Glasgow through the night. I'm right behind the driver whose seat seems to be on shock absorbers, moving up and down in front of me all the while. I've prepared beforehand but the forced insomnia presses in on me. I'm going round in circles thinking of the great information theorist S.R. Ranganathan and his five laws of librarianship:

1. Books are for use.
2. Every person his or her book.
3. Every book its reader.
4. Save the time of the reader.

But what on earth is the fifth? The first four laws just repeat, to the improvisatory rhythm of the pneumatic seat in front of me.

The bus lets us all off at the site of the disused train depot next to the old St Pancras Hotel, which is almost in ruins itself. I don't know it, but ten years later the building that replaces that goods yard will be the new British Library. St Pancras, in time, will be transformed, too.

I make my way across London on foot then settle at a little café off the Strand, gulping down coffee after coffee to stay awake. Finally I head off to face the panel.

They're in a meeting room in an upstairs room within Whitehall itself. All in something like their Sunday best, one asks me a gentle question to begin with – 'How was your journey? Did you fly or take the train?'.

Then they ask me questions with a gravity which seems as theological as technical. One lady looks at me with a kind of trembling fervency and asks 'So Mr Price, would you say you were more of an Indexer than a Classifier?' The question is resonant with shibboleth and grudge. I am afraid I have wandered into a religious trap that would locate me on the wrong side of a centuries-old dispute. I look beyond her, out of the window, and see the top of a London plane tree in the first green exuberance of Spring. I remember the fifth law. 'Well,' I begin, '*The library is a growing organism*, so you could say it's all a matter of... of context in the... the ecosystem.'

Whatever the rest of my answer is (as with many interviewees, the shock of the process erases the memory of much of the experience) I clearly pass muster. The Commission write to me within a few days to tell me that they are 'pleased to recommend me' to the British Library, and the Library duly write a few days after that, claiming me as one of their own.

Later I hear the Stromness job went to a Londoner. To me, that makes a kind of cosmic sense.

Czesław Miłosz: Trapped in Dark Times

TONY ROBERTS

Standing in the ruins of St John's Cathedral in Warsaw on a spring day in 1945, Czesław Miłosz asked himself what he was doing there: 'You swore never to be / A ritual mourner'. At the time the poem was written, however, he felt his duty was inescapable, for like Antigone's the circumstances were 'beyond the power of endurance'.

During forty comfortable years of California 'exile', Miłosz grew to feel trapped by 'this burden'. He lived in a globe of his Polish years: a poet-witness to the horrors of the Second World War, a prose anti-communist of the Cold War. What freed him was the award of the Nobel Prize in Literature in October 1980. The acclaim lessened the criticism of his years of serving (or of renouncing) the communist Republic of Poland. The award chimed with the times. Poland had been made 'fashionable' by the 1978 election of a Polish pope (John Paul II) and the establishment of 'Solidarity', Poland's first independent trade union.

Suddenly acknowledged a major poet, Miłosz would conclude his later book-length *Conversations* with Ewa Czarnecka and Aleksander Fiut by describing how he felt that the label 'historical poet' made him uncomfortable, because 'the proportions are distorted'. He preferred to acknowledge another self: 'the meditative poet'. 'Everything we've been talking about,' he said, 'may be reducible to my discomfort when my image is too noble.'

This same frustration was spelt out less equably in Miłosz's letter to the *New York Review of Books* (2 June 1988) in response to a long, admiring review by Al Alvarez of *The Collected Poems, 1931–1987*: 'You may guess my uneasiness when I saw the long evolution of my poetic craft encapsuled by Mr. Alvarez in the word "witness," which for him is perhaps a praise, but for me is not'. He felt that in citing poems relating to the war, or from his books *The Captive Mind* (*Zniewolony umysł*, 1953) and *Native Realm: A Search for Self-Definition* (*Rodzinna Europa*, 1959), the critic had embalmed him. He went on to say, 'we should distinguish between our duty to preserve memory and our natural desire to move forward with our affairs of the living'.

Yet Miłosz's years of productivity in California had done little to dissuade the world that his finest hours as a writer were spent on the experience of his first forty years or so. His work frequently returned to Central Europe's darkest days which, in conversation, he acknowledged: 'Poland was in the very eye of the cyclone, the lowest depths of the German occupation in Europe. To a large extent my later work is an attempt to deal with that experience. Not only mine as an individual, but the entire collective's experience.'

He had been born in Szetejnie, Lithuania, a part of Tsarist Russia in 1911. His family – dispossessed gentry – were Polish and Lithuanian. Miłosz attended local Catholic schools in Wilno (Vilnius), a Polish-Jewish city with a strong Russian presence, which lacked a 'healthy economic basis'. Miłosz was both poor and conflicted. In *Native Realm* he is a highly self-critical, independent and arrogant figure, idealistic yet filled with the aggressive certainty of Catholic teaching.

At Stefan Batory University he suffered 'a sort of religious crisis'. There he began publishing poems and joined literary groups. In order to experience something of the world, he and two friends undertook a gruelling, often humiliating trip to Paris in 1931, where he met his cousin, Oskar Miłosz. The older Miłosz wrote poetry in French in which he celebrated his Lithuanian background. His conversation, Miłosz reckoned, 'inclined me toward the apocalyptic'.

He wrote of it in *Native Realm*: 'The poems I wrote then did not call for revolutionary action, but there was terror in them and a foreboding'. These were the 'gloomy visions of our so-called "catastrophists school"'. The poetry of social protest he dismissed as mere journalism, though he also tried to write it, 'to redeem myself for not taking part in the workers' clashes with the police'. Miłosz would move left, while the extreme Right would eventually join the underground Home Army; one reason for his distancing himself from taking up arms during the war.

In 1933 he published his first collection of poetry, *Poem on Frozen Time (Poemat o czasie zastygłym)*. He graduated with a degree in law the following year, even though 'Law was the department for people who didn't know what to do with themselves'. In Paris again in 1935, this time with a grant from the National Cultural Fund, Miłosz attended the Alliance française. He would always love France (while his primary feeling towards America would be gratitude). At this time a great influence on him was the thought of the French Catholic philosopher Jacques Maritain. Miłosz would come to attribute his objectivity and neoclassical decorum to his Catholic upbringing.

Upon his return to Wilno, he worked unhappily as a programmer for Polish radio. In that year he published his second collection, *Three Winters* (Trzy zimy), but was subsequently fired for leftist views. He travelled to Italy, then resumed his career in Warsaw in the planning office of Polish radio, where he met his future wife, Janina (Janka) Cękalska. As he later told Fiut, 'All Warsaw seemed tense to me. A fast, cunning city.' Miłosz continued to publish in magazines there, though later confessing to having been a 'lost soul'. When the war came he was already twenty-eight years old. Fortunately he had served his poetic apprenticeship with some acclaim.

With the Nazi invasion of Poland on 1 September 1939, Polish Radio's HQ evacuated. He and Janka were separated. He had been recuperating from flu in eastern Poland and Janka had returned to her parents outside Warsaw. The following summer the Red Army arrived in Wilno. In order to reunite with her, he arranged his escape from the city by a dangerous, circuitous route to Nazi-occupied Warsaw. They joined the socialist resistance, though Miłosz's involvement would be largely literary. In *A Treatise on Poetry* (1957) he would write:

The twenty-year-old poets of Warsaw
Did not want to know that something in this century
Submits to thought, not to Davids with their slings.

During the occupation he focused on underground projects (readings, translations, theatre, lectures, publishing). At one point, he and Jerzy Andrzejewski began an underground periodical. The Miłoszs, like others, busied themselves in the black market (cigarettes and whisky). Then he found employment as a janitor at the Warsaw University Library, where he salvaged war-damaged books in the Polish Academy of Sciences.

He reckoned that the time he spent there, from 1941 to 1943, accounted for a good part of his intellectual development. The war focused his subject and gave him a perspective on it: 'By fusing individual and historical elements in my poetry,' he wrote, 'I had made an alloy that one seldom encounters in the West.' Also, as his *Guardian* obituary noted, 'The experience in Warsaw under the occupation purified his language and imagery'.

On 1 August 1944 the Warsaw Uprising began, which inspired his 'Campo dei Fiori', turning on a surreal, though real, carousel:

The bright melody drowned
the salvos from the ghetto wall,
and couples were flying
high in the cloudless sky.

Terrible weeks followed until the Miłoszs escaped to friends in Goszyce, near Kraków. It was their good fortune to have reliable, influential friends appear in their life at the most difficult times.

To deal with what he had seen in those traumatic weeks, Miłosz adopted an accessible, observer's perspective (at whatever psychological cost). According to his own *The History of Polish Literature* (1969), 'When a poet is overwhelmed by strong emotions, his form tends to become more simple and more direct':

I hear voices, see smiles. I cannot
Write anything; five hands
Seize my pen and order me to write
The story of their lives and deaths.
'In Warsaw'

Some measure of the scope of his thinking during the war is provided in *Legends of Modernity: Essays and Letters from Occupied Poland, 1942–1943*. In his preface Miłosz saw these essays as 'an attempt to clear the field of convictions about man's natural impulses' and its value as 'something of an intellectual memoir' in 'dark times'. 'What stands out in them,' he asserted, 'is a critical stance against nationalism... and a defence of realism in art.' He had moved, he wrote in one of the letters, 'from absolute historicism and Marxist interests toward Catholicism or, rather, toward lay religiosity'.

At the war's end the couple moved to Kraków. Miłosz resumed a public profile, immediately joining the Writers' Union and establishing a literary magazine,

Creativity (*Twórczość*). His collected poems, *Rescue* (*Ocalenie*), were published by the state publishing house. He also contributed a controversial newspaper column to *Dziennik Polski*, a paper backed by the new regime. He had joined the Polish diplomatic service in the hope of an enlightened socialist programme. However, fearing the idea of a Soviet life in Poland, he petitioned friends for a diplomatic posting.

Later it became necessary for Miłosz's peace of mind and for his credentials as an anti-communist to explain his actions. He did this in *The Captive Mind*, where he explained: 'I served abroad because I was thus relieved from direct pressure and, in the material which I sent to my publishers, could be bolder than my colleagues at home. I did not want to become an émigré and so give up all chance of taking a hand in what was going on in my own country.' He had, of course, underestimated his ideological enemy: 'what was planned in Moscow as a stage on the road to servitude, was willingly accepted in the countries concerned as though it were true progress':

What is poetry which does not save
Nations or people?
A connivance with official lies,
A song of drunkards whose throats will be cut
in a moment,
Readings for sophomore girls.

'Dedication'

In 1946 Miłosz took a diplomatic post, first in New York and then Washington. He maintained contacts with the Polish literary press, though he felt hypocritical in his role as the Second Secretary at the Embassy of People's Poland. There were compensations. For one thing, he found the air of America exhilarating after the melancholy of Poland's. A brief return home in 1949 alarmed him at the state of the nation. The following year Miłosz was transferred to the embassy in Paris. Although useful as a literary figure, he was increasingly distrusted by the state. Recalled home briefly, he finally defected in Paris, fearing the situation and the compromises he was making. His decision, he said, proceeded from 'the revolt of the stomach'.

In hiding for several months, Miłosz was supported by the magazine *Kultura*. His was the Paris of the intellectuals, but not of the fashionable set. Of its vogue for existentialism and communism he wrote, 'They were just talking in their sleep'. He was further aware that the West would continue to misunderstand, as Milan Kundera would explain in a *New York Review of Books* piece from April 1984, that Central Europe needed to 'preserve their Westernness' against Soviet hegemony, that Europe was to them a spiritual not a geographical notion, tying them to civilisation.

Ironically, *The Captive Mind* highlighted Miłosz's former communism. McCarthyism made his return to America problematic. The family reunited in 1953, when Janka and the children joined him in France. They bought a house in Montgeron, a suburb of Paris in 1957, and in 1960 Miłosz accepted a teaching position at the University of California, Berkeley, in the Department of Slavic Languages and Literature. Twenty years later came his Nobel Prize for Literature and international celebrity. Welcomed home, he died in 2004 in Krakow, a celebrated figure.

The positive reception accorded the recently published *Poet in the New World: Poems, 1946–1953* indicates that the focus of critical interest in Miłosz's work remains on the first half of his life. In the poem I began with, 'In Warsaw', written at the war's end, he feared what might become his lifelong discomfort:

Was I born to become
a ritual mourner?
I want to sing of festivities,
The greenwood into which Shakespeare
Often took me.

The answer is that there would be many festivities, but the hold this major poet has on posterity is Antigone's.

Granada

JAMES WOMACK

'I don't care to look back. The human history is not so hot.'
Zero Mostel

When I was big and you were little,
I sang a different song. An isolated
sundial pointer tells me it is night.
I'm here for the dawn, a dark hour's climbing
to be ready for that slow inundation.

As easy as saying 'let there be light',
but you need to know what light is first.
The double-glazed silence over the landscape,
this yellow late summer landscape.
A walk through our controlled-burn future.

Of course, it is useless to write a poem
that is, more or less, 'Standing in the Alhambra
on the day of Worrying Election Results'.
Reality is a battle you've lost;
reality is not exhausted by facts.

Elsewhere, everywhere elsewhere,
seagulls fly over a trash monoculture.
We're constantly forced to the breach,
while the best part of the world is a garden
seen through a curved stone arch.

So, we're all at the border. *La frontière est partout.*
We have shown ourselves to be barbarians,
fanatics, extremists who so dread the future.
It's natural, a harbour remembers better
the ships that arrive than the ships that depart.

This is the best coffin I've ever been in.
The standard recipe for the philosopher's stone –
take of spayne clere light is how it begins.
All I've had to eat today is fingernails and ibuprofen.
The sun comes up, which is a joy, considering.

'I hope you're well, no longer grieving,
or not quite as much... I'm on a holiday in my own life.
I hope you're not dead in your bed somewhere,
not with the weather so nice...' *Beep.*
I hang up the phone, know I've not said everything.

I feel dumb today, with a dumb black pencil.
Drawing is an act of the intelligence,
but cut me and I only bleed emojis.
Here's one: a skeleton wearing braces;
here's one: a cat with human hands.

You're trying to intellectualise something.
Desperately. And you're wasting your time.
'Daddy?'
          'Yes?'
                    'Remember your grannies are dead.'
Heredity, that mysterious science
which does not know where it begins, or ends.

At the top of the palace hill, panting
the provocative ozone, I recite to myself:
'Who then inherits the mortal world –
The world with its coming and going,
The world that ends with death?'

A man has appeared in this illusory world
and disturbed the peaceful lives of the tribe.
Was winning Granada like winning Troy,
when losing it was losing Paradise?
If the world's too sweet and living too dear...

The man assured us he wasn't a stranger,
he said in fact he was somebody he knew.
I wish I could change the things I already changed.
Down the hill, which was a bugger to climb,
the city shines bright as an offshore casino.

The past resembles the future
more than one drop of water another;
when you feed your dead I take the meat from their hands.
I opened my eyes and saw the world
crowded with heroes on grey-dappled horses.

'Oh no! History! My one weakness!'
A child clutches his heart in mock distress:
great art is comic, among the cosmic dust.
A black cat playing with a mouse is History.
Deadwhelp history is done for, with its excesses.

Before I started to investigate middens
I thought no hill could be made of ash,
but after a summer with the pomegranates
and the sadomasochistic rosehips
my heart is clean and my mind is changed.

A black dog, like the ragged silhouette
of a black dog, crouches behind me
and I hear my wife say 'Nobody moans
as much as you do, apart from Ovid'.
I don't mind being stepped on by the journey.

Where others may see a trap,
I see the sovereignty of chance.
¿Os movéis para ver muertos?
¿No tenéis espejos por ventura?
I ask the sun for advice and get an answer.

What is this so sickeningly like?
What is this exactly like in my former life?
I don't want any of your songs.
I just want to remember things.
I taught you Christianity, my failed boy.

There was a letter from my brother, who asked:
'The life you are living, right now... What evidence
will there be for it, at a future date?'
All the large houses suddenly collapsed.
All the small houses remained standing.

The very idea that despair has a vocabulary:
even the best cooks are stymied when their ingredients
are reduced to shoe-leather and sleet.
Time has taken away the concept of a soul;
replaced it with a what-will-the-neighbours-say.

Perhaps the real terrorists were the friends
we made along the way, flattering an empty present
with an exaggerated past. It is possible
to have an objectively 'good' life
and still feel sad most of the time.

To name the living world is a responsibility.
She wipes her mouth like someone cleaning silver,
the god whose death sets violence in motion.
There are corners to everything;
there are hidden corners to the river.

A dark well down which she fell back.
(Even here a telephone, private, unlisted,
rang continuously, unknown.)
Behind will be terror; in front of us
the city of the resurrection.

Not everything true should be made public.
Even God has secrets, and the urging present
is not always sober. I went softly towards my god
who softly whistled, as innocent as a Catholic
schoolgirl sitting on the Pope's lap.

And the dead god at the table across from me
refused to acknowledge me, and wiped her mouth.
Why is so much done so many times?
The people who lived in glass houses
have seen a great light...

When I was big and you were little,
I sang, and kept singing, a different song.
'Who then inherits the mortal world –
The world with its coming and going,
The world that ends with death?'

'Who then inherits the mortal world –
The world with its coming and going,
The world that ends with death?'
Some day you too will come in from the rain.
'Who then inherits ...?'

[Womack Out]

God's Day

SINÉAD MORRISSEY

Hope you're okay over there in Belfast. It looks terrible on the news.

My English pen pal was the daughter of my mother's old best friend in New Whittington. I was reading this, her latest missive, up a tree in our back field. I'd scratched my knees on my way up. I was always scratching my knees. My knees wore permanent dark brown patches, as though they'd been mended badly. My English pen pal, who was two years older than me and about to go off the rails with drink and boys, sounded very concerned.

Petrol bombs and riots. Men starving themselves to death. It must be awful.

From up here, you could see our washing line, my mother's dresses blowing beside the tea towels. You could see our patio and coal bunker and the expanse of the back field and the tennis courts hardly anyone played tennis on and Dalriada Hall. Lectures over for another year, the students had all gone home. Apart from the occasional security guard doing his rounds, dressed in black like an Enid Blyton policeman, I had the campus to myself.

It's so hard for us here in England to understand – murdering each other over religion.

The sea winked at me through the tree's foliage. Mostly Belfast Lough was grey to match the sky (*the clouds so low they're sittin on the ground*, lamented my Great Aunt Donnell, my Irish granny's sister, whose real name was Margaret, though nobody called her that). But this bright June Saturday the sea was blue, pointing the long finger of itself in towards the shipyards. Belfast Lough was too polluted to swim in and too stony to paddle. But it didn't matter. It was still brilliant, having the sea on your doorstep. My brother and I would trip across the Shore Road to fly kites or walk out to the end of the barnacle-crusted sewage pipe or tip rocks over scouring for crabs. County Down sat across from us, practically close enough to touch. To our left, at the mouth of the Lough, lay Scotland. *Mull of Kintyre, oh mist rolling in from the sea, my desire is always to be here, oh Mull of Kintyre...* my English granny would croon after a Guinness, whereas my Irish granny only sang songs about Ireland. On principle.

We're so lucky where we live, not growing up in a war.

Later we'd go for a swim, over in the Poly's main building. While my parents ploughed lengths, Conor and I would muck about in the diving pool, which was dark and cold and bottomless, taking turns bombing off the diving boards. We'd buy packets of Tayto Cheese 'n' Onion crisps from the Sports Centre reception and eat them on the way home.

Please write back and let me know that you're safe.

What on earth did she mean?

I was as safe as I'd ever be. I was so safe on the Poly campus that for years after I left, most of my dreams still happened there, the back field and the tennis courts and the sea their unwavering backdrop.

*

Just as the Falklands War was about to, the Troubles unfolded exclusively on television. Adults-in-miniature, my brother and I watched whatever our parents watched, left alone to decipher the random bits of pixelated world beamed into our living room for ourselves.

Because being a communist meant following the news, the news was on all the time. We watched Sean Rafferty on *Scene around Six.* Photographs of people who'd been killed that day – young guys on their wedding day, RUC officers in uniform – would cut to a journalist in a beige duffel coat holding a fluffy microphone.

'Around 7.30 am this morning...' he'd intone, out on some freezing by-road. Behind him, staked off with police tape, a mangle of detonated metal that had recently been somebody's car.

Sometimes the journalist would be filmed outside a court house. Or a prison. Long-haired men in blankets had been on television for a while, standing in front of windows, light falling across their faces. They looked like Jesus. When the camera lingered on the walls behind them, I knew it was trying to show me something, but I wasn't sure what.

Funerals aplenty. People standing six-deep along the road. Helicopters overhead. Men in army uniforms with balaclavas and sunglasses firing rifles into the sky. Black flags. Flags of the Irish Republic. Flowers. Gloves. Boys in miniature suits. Girls in white tights and patent leather shoes. Police stations like citadels. Low brown hills evaporating into clouds.

The television held all kinds of surprises. We also watched *Life on Earth* and *The Kenny Everett Video Show* and *Wimbledon.* We also watched *Carry on Camping* and *Of Human Bondage* and *Picnic at Hanging Rock.* To me, the 1981 Hunger Strike was as mysterious and far away as three girls vanishing into a crevice in Australia under sway of an invisible force.

*

One summer, my mother off on a Communist Party jaunt to the Soviet Bloc, my father took my brother and me by boat and meandering train to London.

'Let's get some eggs and throw them at 10 Downing Street', he suggested.

My father was used to throwing things at Conservatives. He'd once travelled to Brighton with a friend to throw stones at Ministers during the Conservative Party Conference. When the police set their dogs after them, down at the pebbly beach, my father's friend just picked up more stones and clubbed the dogs over the head. Lithe and lucky, my father beat a fleet retreat. The law loved my father. He didn't know why. Called as a witness, he'd once confessed in the dock to the crime of organising an illegal civil rights march himself, and still didn't get arrested.

When we arrived at Downing Street there was a police barrier. We couldn't get close enough to throw anything. *Thank you God, thank you God,* I muttered under my breath. Without bulletproof vests or weapons, the police looked weirdly undressed.

We went on ordinary excursions too. The London Dungeon. London Zoo. Trailed from bookshop to bookshop.

'Daddy's written a book!' shrieked my brother, discovering one with my father's name on it, mortifying him.

We rode Double Decker buses and ate lamb cutlets in Greek restaurants, whose sweet-talking waiters carried white towels over their forearms.

One evening we passed a burning car. Conor and I turned our heads and gawped at it. People stood back and watched, as though burning cars in England were a common fixture. My brother and I couldn't stop staring. The air around the car melted and pulsed. The hood was already black and flames were shooting out of the windows. I hurried closer to my father and took his hand.

'Haven't you seen a car on fire before?' he asked, genuinely surprised.

Northern Ireland was on fire. Northern Ireland had been on fire since we were born. But, as far as we were aware, this was the first real-life burning car my brother and I had ever witnessed.

My father didn't bat an eye. He'd seen plenty of burning cars. Had maybe set fire to cars himself, under orders from his father, manning the Turf Lodge barricades, and gotten away scot-free.

*

We moved house semi-regularly. I grew used to the architecture of my life collapsing in the time it took to drive a car out of a driveway. Or later, for a person to put on their coat and walk out the door, and for the family left behind to implode. With each move, we existed in a slightly altered relationship to the Troubles, my parents growing more prosperous, more removed from the immediate bloodshed, as I got older.

I was too young to remember much about our first house, a pebbledash semi on an estate outside Lurgan under Provisional IRA control. Here the conflict had saturated our lives, had poured in through the doors and windows like floodwater. Years afterwards, my mother filled me in.

'They shot the postman for delivering letters stamped with the head of the Queen. They shot rival Republicans. Of course they shot soldiers all the time. I felt sorry for the radio operators. You'd see them straggling along at the back of patrols with their big heavy equipment, antennae waving. They may as well have had *shoot me* written across their backs.'

In Lurgan, land of two-babies-in-nappies-and-no-washing-machine, my mother had been young, poor, lonely, and English.

'Two men called to the door. I knew what they'd come for. I knew they had guns hidden in their jackets. But they didn't ask for your father. They asked for someone else. *Oh,* your father said, *he doesn't live here.* Then they just moved off down the street, looking for this other man. Quakers turned up to try and help for a while but they soon left. It was insane.'

'You don't remember the Army banging us awake at all hours?' asked my father, as though I'd been born with full adult consciousness.

'Provos on the run slipping in through our back door, dandling you on their knee, pretending to be your father, while I went out for a walk? Soldiers barging in barking questions, turning the house upside down? I suppose you don't remember any of this?'

I was two years old.

I remember a rag doll and a rubber plant called George.

I remember a railway crossing by a graveyard, angels and Virgin Marys behind a grey stone wall, lifting their broken hands. Smoke from my mother's cigarettes, snaking upwards. My mother sweeping me onto the countertop for no reason. *You're my little honey pie,* she said, kissing the top of my head, and I overran with joy. From Lurgan, my brother first went to school, on the bus by himself, to P1 at St Theresa's, where more Virgin Marys stood about the grounds. I crawled and walked and talked and my mother got a job as a waitress in The Manhattan. As soon as I could speak, I asked my father the same question.

'Where's Mummy?'

'Run off with a soldier.'

I knew exactly what this soldier looked like. Young (they were all young) and blonde. He had a machine gun.

*

In 1975, we upped and moved to the Rathmore estate in Craigavon, into a split-level council house in wild vermillion casing, five floors full, the eyes of its windows in peculiar places. The move was a no-brainer for my parents. A New Town slung between Catholic Lurgan and Protestant Portadown, mixed, cheap, semi-rural, marked by innovative Scandinavian design and the inspiration (apparently) behind Milton Keynes, Craigavon promised relative riches. We would never live in such a tall house again, each room stacked on top of another room on a storey all its own, like a house in a nursery rhyme.

In Craigavon days began to happen consecutively. As I grew steadier on my feet, ran, skipped, sang and spouted baggy, hairbrained sentences, my sense of time passing grew solid, fully flexed. Memories, previously islanded in haze, began to expand, so that breakfast connected now both to waking up in my bedroom beforehand, and going out afterwards with my mother to the shops at Legahory. Time, after a bumpy beginning, rolled forwards.

On my first day of school, my mother walked me to the gates of Tullygally Primary and then promptly walked away. I stood about aimlessly on the playground wondering what to do next.

'Are you lost?' asked a kind lady, possibly the receptionist, as she approached me across the tarmac. I nodded. She took me by the hand. 'Here, let me take you over to your classroom.'

On our way we passed kids, luminous with snot, clinging to their mothers' legs. Why were their mothers even here? Inside the building was even worse. Girls rushing off to the toilets, coming back with their tights round their ankles, utterly undone by the uniform. Or wetting themselves. Or throwing up where they stood. A year before, when I was three, I'd walked to and from nursery school every day by myself. Nursery had been a large hall with a green wooden door at the end of our street. And though I'd lain on the floor once during nap time and watched the Honey Monster from the Sugar Puff advert materialise through the ceiling, shaggy outline first, then face, then body, until the whole grinning bulk of him had hung suspended above my head, nursery had never been as cacophonous as this.

'Who loves you?' asked our teacher, Miss Wilson, once the strange mothers had been dispatched and we'd been assigned our seats with our names on the desk in front of us and settled down. My parents loved me. My brother loved me. But it turned out God loved me too. Who was God? God was watching. God was in our hearts. God was sunshine, cheery as the yellow flower painted on the playground wall outside. After lunch, we sang a song God got mixed up in. *When the Big Ship Sailed on the Alley Alley O on the Last Day of September*, God was in the engine room, God was jamming the works, God was waiting in the black water.

'God doesn't exist', said my father matter-of-factly when I got home. 'The Capitalists made God up.'

'Don't forget to go to church on Sunday', called Miss Wilson one Friday afternoon as we steamrolled towards the door. I thought she was talking to me. I thought this a specific instruction. With my innate fear of authority, I always did what adults told me, but this instruction threw me into a quandary. I would have to go, because Miss Wilson had told me to go, but I also knew, aged five, that I would have to go in secret because my parents could never find out.

That Sunday after breakfast I got carefully dressed (I am stumped trying to imagine what my notion of *carefully dressed* might have been – my school shoes? My birthday gown?) and left by the back door. My parents wouldn't worry or wonder where I was. Barring mealtimes and bedtime, my brother and I were free to roam wherever we wanted.

The white church near the shops was dull and sombre. It looked like some kind of meeting room. No Virgin Marys here. No anything really. Dark wooden pews and wide plain windows. I'd made an awful mistake. Miss Wilson hadn't meant *me.* This place had nothing to do with *me.* But I'd got myself there, on time as it turned out, and it seemed too late now to leave. And so I sat down beside a straitjacketed family of four through the long drone of the service, the hymns I didn't know, the sermon I didn't understand, burning up, crackling, with the shame of it. The shame not of sin, but of stupidity.

If the Capitalists made God up, in Craigavon the differences between Protestants and Catholics still started to claim my attention. The understanding that these differences were real, and vitally important, was a kind of atmosphere, seeping in through the cracks and crannies of my disjunctive family. I couldn't escape it.

Legend had it that my father's mother, Catherine, my Irish granny, had baptised me in her kitchen sink in case I died early of some infant ailment and ended up in limbo. Does it work if your granny baptises you? Does it work if she means well? *I claim you for Christ our Saviour by the sign of His cross. I now trace the cross on your forehead...* The sink in my granny's kitchen was narrow. Holding me *and* the holy water, keeping one hand free for signs, took deft manoeuvring. At least I wouldn't have cried, even if I'd been surprised by the cold water. According to my mother, I never cried. When I arrived home after an inexplicably pain-free delivery (*I fell asleep*, said my mother, *and when I woke up I just wanted to push*) I slept straight through the night, and every night thereafter. Two spoonfuls of sugar water and a quick flip onto my side had worked miracles.

'I love my country and I love my church.'

My Irish granny stated her allegiances in strict order. A card-carrying member of the Party, Communism never featured on the list – a borrowed theology from her husband she wore lightly. Whenever she had my brother and me to herself, she'd take us to down to the Marian Grotto on Castle Street, lift us up to the statue of the Virgin Mother and make us kiss Her feet. The Grotto was a fawn cave in dim shadow and Our Lady stood sculpted into the wall, as though She was standing inside a shell. She wore a robe of pale, worn turquoise, the colour of a faded sky. Perhaps She'd been dipped in the colour of Heaven but lost half Her pigment on her journey back to earth. Perhaps Heaven itself was half-hearted. The foot-kissing freaked me out, but not nearly as much as the inside of the chapel, its smoky smell, its candles for the departed, Jesus both dead on a cross and alive in a flickering painting, holding His chest apart.

After the move to Craigavon, Conor left St Theresa's and joined me in Tullygally Primary. He never attended a Catholic school again, and as I never attended a Catholic school, but four State schools in quick succession, I believed my brother had begun his education in a foreign country. Not that we felt at home with the *de-facto* Protestantism of the State sector either. But at least from now on we would be estranged from the same things, and at the same time.

In Rathmore, two kids roughly our age lived next door. For a while we walked to school together. Their father was a Minister. His collar confused me. I tried not to stare at it. Their house was exactly the same as our house but had a different smell. Daz and Jiff and Johnson and Johnson's baby powder. Twins lived in a play pen in the kitchen. Where we had riotous colours on our walls our parents had painted themselves – mustard in the living-room, indigo in the bedroom my brother and I shared – the walls of the Minister's house were white. One Sunday morning, Conor and I knocked on their front door. It didn't open.

'Hello?' called a voice from the hall.

'Are you coming out to play?'

'I can't come out', said the boy.

'Why not?'

'Because it's God's day.'

His dark eyes blinked at us through the letterbox.

God's day? How could God own a day? A day wasn't even a thing.

We didn't walk to school as often together after that. In the general exodus out of the estate as Rathmore began to disintegrate, their family was the first to leave.

*

'I'm sure that barman in Lurgan yesterday slipped me a Micky Finn.'

Once a year, my English granny would materialise off the Liverpool ferry like Captain Kirk in *Star Trek* and stay for a month. She lived in the boxroom at the top of the house, up four flights of stairs, with a blind instead of curtains. On sunny afternoons while my granny napped, trapped heat would intensify and beat its wings. Over the double bed hung a map of Ireland made of pints of Guinness, my granny's favourite drink. The map had no border. The whole of Ireland swam together in a froth of foam. England was nowhere in sight. Each morning she folded her neat, widow's body into a metal orthopaedic corset with hanging straps for stockings and lodged her feet inside sensible shoes. My granny, my mother and I were having breakfast (or *break fast* as my granny called it, because you're *breaking* your night-time *fast*). My mother handed me a plate of toast and a cup of Lapsang Souchong. My granny poured her ordinary tea into her saucer and blew on it.

'You're imagining things.'

'I know he did. He gave me a funny look – just after he heard me talk. I knew as soon as we got back I wasn't right. It was fine for you. You were going out with Michael. But I had to stay and look after the children and I couldn't keep my eyes open. I could hardly move. My legs were a tonne weight. It took all my strength to get those two upstairs and into bed. I'm telling you Hazel. It wasn't normal.'

My granny came from New Whittington where we went on our summer holidays. New Whittington put me to sleep, with its old people's flats, where my granny lived, and inland, airless weather. *To woo you, to woo you,* cooed the woodpigeons in the poplar trees near the allotments.

Whenever I spoke it sounded strange, as though my voice was a bell, or I'd been shoved underwater. In New Whittington nothing happened. In Craigavon, everything happened so fast it was hard to keep up. Though she loved Guinness, and green was her favourite colour, and her maiden name had been Coffey, meaning someone up the line in her family had originally hailed from Cork, my granny was continually perplexed by the strangeness of where her daughter had landed, with its bomb scares and riots on the television and hideous Mickey Finns.

'We don't have women called Donnell in England', she'd offer as an example.

*

'What are you?' asked a kid, knocking Coke bottles over with stones in the concrete playground behind our house.

'I'm half English and half Irish.'

Dangling off a wall by my fingertips, I imagined the two halves of my body filled with differently coloured blood. It wasn't what he meant.

'Do you go to church?'

'No.'

'Do you go to chapel?'

'No.'

'But what *are* you then? You must be something.'

I shrugged. I had no idea.

He stopped knocking the bottles over and stared at me, confused.

It never occurred to me at the time I could ask him anything back.

*

Money Money Money. ABBA were number one forever and Elvis was dead inside the television. The Flintstones were dead inside the television too, had died millions of years ago at the time of the dinosaurs, but had somehow kept going, sprightly in their Stone-Age clothes. Rupert the Bear travelled into the television on a shaft of afternoon sunlight, sparkly with dust.

Some things were easy and some things were hard. Chess was easy. I set the board up right first time. Reading was easy. Miss Wilson quickly took away *Play with Us* and gave me *Read and Write* instead. Adding up without using my fingers was hard. Subtraction, even if I used my fingers, was hard. Running to the shop for a 5p mix-up was hard. Gangs of teenagers hung out along the way, smoking. You never knew what they'd do to you.

'Arms up in space', said my mother at bedtime, helping me off with my jumper.

I was already up so high, space was within touching distance, crackly and furiously fast, though in summer it stayed bright for an age and space would fail to appear. I'd lie awake then, listening to the estate. Dogs. Fights. Sirens. Some boy taking an hour to kick a can along the back alley.

At any one time in Craigavon during the 1970s thousands of houses stood empty. The Development Commission had built too many, high on notions of rivalling Belfast, and by the time we moved in, had resorted to paying families £300 to relocate. £300 which would be quickly pocketed, only for tenants to move out again within weeks, back to their familiar neighbourhoods, where their mothers and cousins and comrades-in-arms were. On certain Craigavon streets there were so many abandoned houses it was as if a neutron bomb had exploded, vaporising humans but leaving their belongings intact.

Teenagers had a field day first. Smashing windows and doors. Dragging mattresses and blankets outside and setting them on fire. When they'd grown bored and moved on to the next house, Conor and I and our posse of littler Rathmore kids moved in. Stuff lay scattered about. Loft insulation. Skipping ropes. Ice-cream scoops. Wires. *On the hillside stands a lady,* we sang, turning a big rope between two of us in an echoey living room while our friends jumped in and out. *Who she is I do not know.* We flicked taps on and off, played hide and seek, did handstands against the walls with our shoes on. I came home for tea one evening with my face dripping blood, though I couldn't remember cutting it, and when my brother trod on a nail in the attic of a derelict house, he casually watched his shoe fill with crimson and didn't say a word.

With so much property to spare, they rehoused 'problem' families from England. A couple from Leeds moved in across the road and the man threw the woman through a downstairs window, leaving the outline of her body in the partially shattered glass, like a cartoon. They rehoused Vietnamese Boat People, who were not treated well. (*Northern Ireland was scary*, one woman recalled later, having survived the Vietnam War). My best friend's mother stabbed her father with kitchen scissors. My friend went into care.

And yet the Army had no presence on Rathmore and I never saw a soldier. If a boy had a gun, it would be to shoot rabbits and birds, for all the older boys carried rabbits' feet for luck and knew how to hunt. One even brought a hare to our back door one August, shot through the abdomen, as a gift from his father, and my father, up for anything, hung it off the handle of the back door for three days before skinning and stewing it. He carried its heart out to the bin wrapped in newspaper.

England. Ireland. Catholic. Protestant. Such notions took root in my life. But already by the time we lived on Rathmore, the violence of the Troubles appeared duller and further off, like the difference between forked and sheet lightning.

Three Poems

JOHN ROBERT LEE

Spectacular

'I need to find a place to be spectacular'
(Jason Allen-Paisant)

Icarus was no Andean condor
no soaring old soul of upper worlds

no scavenger of holy things
in the ordered chaos of the cosmos/

he rode golden copper light
out of mango groves
into rising sun

of a new world he imagined/

against invocations, against
the signalling heat of his pride

against the interminable inferno of the solar deity

his waxen feathers broke him, against the Andean hills/

Apprentice

It was not dramatic, the sundering, not even clearly memorized –

you worshipped, admired, were besotted
by the genius, a particular grace, that huge gift,

mentorship generous, even sharp-edged dismissals
which put you in your place
among the bric-a-brac of attention's

spectrum, of insistent
demands of the work, of narrowing
portals to time declining –

where did you take the prodigal road
to that far city inheritance

of your own veteran certainties, your separating distances?

Mantra

bird warbling insistently

like a cosmic pilgrim
in the liminal space of overcast

light, under grey shroud
of weather, stillness
of avocado and breadfruit trees,

bird with its imitation
Sanskrit hymn, rooster in echo,
a dog's mourning chant –

up the hill come untranslatable
monotonous dance-hall texts

adding their esoterics to these sacred offices.

Césaire

ALEXANDRA REZA

Aimé Césaire's *Cahier d'un retour au pays natal* (*Return to My Native Land*), first published in 1939, and now reissued as a Penguin classic in John Berger and Anna Bostock's 1969 translation, opens with a speaker surveying a landscape characterised by inertia and flatness, and a town 'flat, displayed, brought down'.[1] The voice looks at it all with desolation. At first, the speaker is himself at a low ebb, emaciated by the harrowing violences of racial capitalism and by his own disdain of the homeland he rejects. The poem stages the thickening of that first person as he overcomes contempt, alienation and anger over the course of a long, free verse meditation on consciousness, life and transformation. By the end of the poem the consciousness is towering, a huge expansion of personhood become planetary, with 'ocean hands',[2] 'the enormous lung of cyclones'[3] and a 'gigantic seismic pulse'.[4] Consciousness and character are plastic here: the speaker is hard to pin down, volatile, emotionally unpredictable. By turns mocking, bitter, angry, desperate and knowing, he impersonates, ventriloquises and rejects the racist stereotypes (both the propositions of formal race philosophy and everyday prejudices) that fix people in place and overdetermine them. He wants to – and does, in the end – break out of the moulds offered by colonial society and its desire to 'tame', as he puts it again and again.

'There are two ways to lose yourself,' Césaire wrote elsewhere, 'by walling yourself up in the particular or by diluting yourself in the universal.'[5] And indeed, for all that the psychic freight of the poem is concentrated around the single speaking consciousness, the poem is also talking about the world, staging a repeated contraction and expansion of scale from single character to whole world. Césaire achieves this not by overloading the speaking voice with representative pressure (making the lyric voice speak *for* Black people everywhere) but by showing how histories of empire and enslavement have rendered the speaking subject already-worldly: 'My name is Bordeaux and Nantes and Liverpool and New York and San Francisco / not a corner of this world but carries my thumb-print / and my heel-mark on the backs of skyscrapers.'[6] The poem summons the 'end of the world', where the world stands for *this world* of violence and inequality: 'ENOUGH OF THIS OUTRAGE!'[7]. And so, the question of escaping colonial enclosure plays out, too, at the level of space and history. The transformation of the voice accompanies a revisioning of the history of racial capitalism that has cast down the speaker and those around him. As his consciousness transforms, the slave ship cracks open and the people it carries rise to their feet.

And they are on their feet the captives [...]
Unexpectedly on their feet
On their feet in the hold
[...]
On their feet at the compass
On their feet before the map
On their feet beneath the stars
And their feet
And
Free[8]

It is worth pausing over the 'on their feet' phrase, not just as an image of defiance and protest, but also because Césaire mobilises this trope of modulated repetition throughout the poem. Phrases repeat and alter, ideas are recalled and constantly revised. From the stasis of the early scenes, the poem's world re-energises and moves, and these repetitions and revisions are one way in which Césaire renders the shifting sands of the world on which the poem insists. The lists and repetitions give this free verse poem its structure and its rhythm. Where the French Communist Party (of which Césaire was a member until 1952) had declared that engaged francophone poets must use the alexandrine to write their poetry, Césaire was strongly against the idea of 'a preestablished form, a ready-made mould into which all the poet has to do is insert their own experience'.[9] And so Césaire's concern with escaping enclosure and prescription surfaces too in his whirling free verse, free association and enormously long sentences that threaten to burst their banks.

Why this interest in flux? Katherine McKittrick has argued that one salient characteristic of colonial understandings of space is that they present themselves as

1 Berger and Bostock, p. 2

2 B&B p. 55

3 B&B p. 56

4 B&B p. 56

5 Il y a deux manières de se perdre: par ségrégation murée dans le particulier ou par dilution dans l'universel.

6 Et je me dis Bordeaux et Nantes et Liverpool et New-York et San-Francisco | Pas un bout de ce monde qui ne porte mon empreinte digitale. (pp. 46–7) B & B p. 20

7 B & B p. 29

8 B&B pp. 61–2

9 Sur la poésie nationale: Une forme preetablie, un moule tout fait dans le quel le poète n'a plus qu'à faire rentrer son expérience, 1995

fixed and unpeopled.[10] McKittrick underlines the element of stability in imperialist world views, because, she argues, imagining space as fixed closes the possibilities for understanding the world as a site of change or, more broadly, for imagining change at all. Frantz Fanon also points out the stasis of colonial space in his account of the colonial city in *Les damnés de la terre*. For Fanon, the colonial world is 'a motionless, manichaeistic world, a world of statues' (*monde compartimenté, manichéiste, immobile, monde de statues*). This provides one answer to the question of what is at stake in Césaire's mercurial poetics of space and character: it inscribes the possibility for social, political, spatial change. The voice calls instead for a 'map of the world made for my use',[11] remembering 'those who invented neither powder nor compass'[12], searching for a way of understanding the world that allows those people to be 'on their feet at the compass / on their feet before the map'.[13] To connect powder and compass is, obviously, to connect colonial technologies of understanding space with violence. The poem takes aim at other European technologies of understanding the world, too, like Reason, who appears at one point in a cameo role and anointed 'wind of the evening': powerful, but invisible and unpredictable. Césaire was influenced by the surrealists' calls for freedom. His partner, Suzanne Césaire, wrote that surrealism was 'ardent, and revolutionary [...] the tightrope of our hope'.[14] The surrealist influences on Césaire's writing are clear not only in his poetic voice's explicit rejection of Reason ('we hate you, you and / your reason') but also in the poem's wider interest in consciousness and the unconscious, in dreaming beyond the bounds of how things already are.

*

Césaire's kinematic language is, in important ways, underwritten by an attempt to name reality in all its strangeness. The poem's linguistic volatility seems to have drawn Berger and Bostock to the translation project. 'Most mainstream political language is inert,' John Berger wrote later, and so 'most public discourse does not face up to reality, is evasive.'[15] It also, of course, presents a challenge to any translator. Berger's own ideas about translation disavowed any simplistic sense of an easy transfer from one language to another, gesturing to a practice that he saw in instead as mediated, motivated, uncertain:

> One reads and rereads the words of the original text in order to penetrate through them to reach, to touch, the vision or experience that prompted them. One then gathers up what one has found there and takes this quivering almost wordless 'thing' and places it behind the language it needs to be translated into. And now the principal task is to persuade the host language to take in and welcome the 'thing' that is waiting to be articulated.[16]

There are questions to be asked here about how the translator should, in this view, apprehend the 'wordless "thing"', but in any case, this account offers a compellingly active vision of the translator's work, so often elided in the anglophone imagination.

Bostock and Berger's strategy to persuade English to welcome Césaire's French is often to render his complex, difficult and deliberately intellectual lines in simple, everyday English – a strategy that frequently takes them towards vocabulary rooted in Germanic or Old English. There are moments when this strategy works brilliantly in bringing Césaire's French all the way into their own English, such as 'I break open the yolk-bag that separates me from myself' (*Je force la membrane vitelline qui me / sépare de moi-même*). The Toussaint L'Ouverture passage is also particularly successful, when Bostock-Berger's pace and rhythm slows down wonderfully to meet Césaire's lingering meditation on the Haitian revolutionary leader's death in a French prison: 'Death describes a shining circle above this man / death is gentle star above his head'.[17] Berger and Bostock 'At the end of the small hours' also works very well as a rendering of the central repetition of the first part of the poem (*Au bout du petit matin*). Other translations have struggled to maintain both the quality of ending and the smallness that the French inscribes. Compare: 'At the brink of dawn'[18], 'At the end of early dawn'[19] and 'At the end of first light'[20]. At other moments, the lowering of the register misses something. Clayton Eshleman and Annette Smith's 'the lustral ship fearlessly advances on the crumbling water' is more compellingly strange and ritualistic than Bostock and Berger's 'the cleansed ship advances fearless upon the caving waters'

10 Katherine McKittrick, *Demonic Grounds: Black Women and the Cartographies of Struggle* (Minneapolis; London: University of Minnesota Press, 2006), p. xiii.

11 ('*mon originale géographie aussi; la carte du monde faite à mon usage, non pas teinte aux arbitraires couleurs des savants, mais à la géometrie de mon sang répandu*'). B&B p. 55

12 B&B p. 44 ('*ceux* qui n'*ont inventé ni la poudre ni la boussole*')

13 B&B p. 62 ('*debout à la boussole / debout à la carte*')

14 'Le Surrealism et nous', *Tropiques*, 1943

15 https://www.londonreviewbookshop.co.uk/podcasts-video/podcasts/aime-cesaire-s-return-to-my-native-land-john-berger-in-conversation-with-david-constantine

16 https://www.theguardian.com/books/2014/dec/12/john-berger-writing-is-an-off-shoot-of-something-deeper

17 B&B p. 21

18 Mireille Rosello and Annie Pritchard, *Notebook of a Return to My Native* Land, 1995

19 Gregson Davis, *Journal of a Homecoming*, 1997

20 A. James Arnold and Clayton Eshleman, *Notebook of a Return to the Native Land*, 2013

(*'le navire lustral s'avancer impavide sur les eaux écroulées*). There are some other qualms. For instance, why omit 'notebook' from the English title? For Césaire the schoolteacher, a *cahier* is an important symbol of experimentation, of trying out ideas, of reversing ideas he had been taught as a student.

But alongside the textual ins and outs of the translation, we need to ask the broader question of what the significance of that translation was by those people at that time, and, next, what it means to re-edit it today. Asked about his decision to leave the country he was born in, and how that related to the translation of a poem about returning home from afar, John Berger was quick to emphasise the privilege of his own departure: a free choice to forsake the country in which he never quite felt at home. Bostock, too, had left the land of her birth – first an émigré from Russia, then a refugee from the Nazis, she was a linguist and a translator who had translated many writers on the internationalist Left including Trotsky, Lenin and Marx. Bostock and Berger had already translated Brecht together, and when it was first published in 1969, theirs was the first English translation of Césaire's poem, which had by then gained such a luminous reputation across the decolonizing world beyond the anglophone. Césaire also insisted that, in his understanding at least, Negritude, the movement for which this poem was so foundational, was a corrective to a colourblind communism and so part of the Left. Writers and poets in French and Portuguese such as André Breton and Mário Pinto de Andrade described the work as 'bubbling oxygen'. As Brent Hayes Edwards has argued, translation was one of the essential ways in which the 'turbine' of the cultures of Black internationalism were lubricated,[21] and Bostock and Berger's work stands as a record of a moment of poetic solidarity in confronting empire.

Today, the poet Jason Allen-Paisant has edited their work to 'rectify mistranslations arising from insufficient familiarity with Martinique's geographical and cultural context' and to 'address terms that required updating'. Notably this edition revises out Berger and Bostock use of the N-word, because, Allen-Paisant argues, the French 'nègre' has more nuance than that English word allows. That is an understandable editorial choice, but it would have been useful to hear at greater length what further corrections have been made. Such a discussion would have allowed us better to understand the Berger-Bostock translation in all its historical specificity, and, in turn, to grasp the difference of our own conjuncture of thinking about the decolonial and language.

One major significance of the poem today remains its ambition and dissidence regarding what political poetry could be. In their Translators' Note, Berger and Bostock say that the 'poem is important because of its thinking content [...] both political and poetic'. What that thinking is, though, and the relationship between the poetic and the political the work establishes, is not easily summarised. The poem is, as should be clear by now, both a direct and clear indictment of slavery, colonialism, racism and racial violence and also a text that rethinks what political poetry could be. Césaire was a critic of orthodoxy and dogmatism, not least on the left. In 1955, the year before Césaire published the final edition the *Cahier,* he participated in a debate with other Marxist poets about how politically engaged poets should write. The anticolonial poet should resist being told how to write and should be allowed 'the right to initiative',[22] he argued. The next year, resigning from the French Communist Party, he reiterated his commitment to this idea of creative 'initiative' and indeed to intellectual and creative autonomy more broadly: 'we can't authorise anyone to do our thinking for us'.[23] The poem dramatises this impulse in staging the shifting consciousness of its speaker, who has to work through the dominant received ideas and racist clichés that surround him in order to achieve a new critical consciousness. Césaire made mistakes – many of his readers and comrades never forgave him for advocating departmentalisation rather than decolonisation for Martinique – but he defended the right to make mistakes: 'We black creators have nothing to gain by enclosing ourselves [...] we are big enough to run the risks and dangers of the great adventure of freedom; this is the price of our poetry, our right to initiative as well as our right to make mistakes'.[24] In our conformist age, such productive tensions between political engagement and individual liberty remain generative.

21 Edwards

22 Sur la poésie nationale: 'Le droit à l'initiative', 1995

23 nous ne puissions donner à personne délégation pour penser pour nous.

24 Sur la poésie nationale, 1995

Alfriston Clergy House

JOSEPH MINDEN

If I can just make this one thing not die,
the clappers in the loft will stop their murders.
A spur of the river, the bargemen.
Downpour, springshine.
A Hue Walker through the reeds coming.
Floodable garden.
Wheatish flame
past the casement guttering.
I have been here a thousand years,
a time before my head formed a house
threaded by bluebottles.

Livewell,
Bidenmorta.
Bread oven,
shovel called peels.
That amazing bread oven.
That huge bed of courgettes.

Continent,
Lovegod.
Greene carpet.
Brand irons, a pair
of creepers, fire, shovell, tongs
and bellowes. Sour milk and chalk.

Rammed chalk. Chalk laid and rammed
down, milk poured over.
Initially, a layer of mould over,
gradually died back,
still areas of green mould on the floor where
the daylight is strongest, feels soft,
looks right but is dead,
no hot core,
downs the visible top layer of chalk,
deepens upon chalk,
moisty,
the wet bone of stones.

Who's that sulking in the corner there?
Long Laurence,
Nine Men's Morris,
inscrutable gridwork kept in the chest,
Thomas Cromwell till he fell out of favour
and slept under a juniper tree:
behold, then did quite well, son of gentry,
an angel touched him,
a cake baked on the coals,
and a cruse of water at his head.

The villagers hate me for my love of timber,
the fact that when I cry I shed thatch
and out fumes sooty smoke.
The oak leaf in the corner,
that's a bit of history, not long after the Great War.
A sprig of oak leaves chosen by my uncle,
Joseph Armitage,
I don't know but

Like a tamping rod blown through the eyebase,
England watched aghast, France became
a sea of black flags.
Rats that survived became flea towns,
evidence of the lifestyle at Brighton,
Napoleon-faced syphilis,
an upsurge of village,
omega-shaped,
grown over with bye-laws.
A garderobe?
Fumigate,
yes.

First, the property at Barmouth in Wales,
Octavia,
Robert
and Hardwicke in hands,
a posy trinity.
Then, yes, the second, Alfriston,
a yeoman farmer, naturally built.

Who's that limping along the lucid Cuckmere?
The Rev. Fred, that undaunted conservationist –
the villagers thought him mad;
Robert Witt:
out sprang The Art Fund,
The Courtauld, typically mute,
some deposit from the First Chimurenga;
the ham Earl of Dorset, spluttering;
commissioners of sewers, muttering;
dearest verycoast,
after the kinges high way to Seaford,
reed-dragging his crested pole.

From the start, a quilt
of radical socialists,
key establishment figures,
traditional landowners
and the Royal Family.
A powerful vision,
its vagueness
its power.

We would, naturally, be asked to restore it,
no indigenous collection, a collaboration
to dress the room,
rather a poser if they mean what then to put it to,
spindly bed frame limp with bonnet curds,
crumpet stale as plastic,
looping letters,
one corner of a central meadow,
twisted spire,
and a ladder to heaven for ever,
river outfall,
the ruynes of an ancient chapple.
Harriet,
keeping chickens in a hollow tree.
Older versions, titans buried under the hill.
Fences adored.
Haunters of silences.
My tongue,
pen
and paintbrush combined.
I have just heard from Mr Loftus Brock.
The present is so obviously imaginary.
Bring out your dead.

From *What Is Poetry?*

PHILIP TERRY

In his poem 'A Daylight Art', dedicated to the poet Norman MacCaig, Seamus Heaney recounts the story of Socrates' last day, where he tells his friends he has been putting Aesop's fables into verse. A dream recurring throughout Socrates' life kept repeating one instruction: *practise the art.* Which until his final day Socrates always took to be philosophy. Heaney concludes:

> Happy the man, therefore, with a natural gift
>
> for practising the right one from the start –
> poetry, say, or fishing; whose nights are dreamless;
> whose deep-sunk panoramas rise and pass
>
> like daylight through the rod's or the nib's eye.

Like Heaney's poem, one of the first pieces of my own writing that meant something to me was a sort of parable, in prose, called 'A Use for Rumney's', and for years I took it as containing a secret instruction: to write fiction. It's now lost, but the story, influenced by reading Kafka's short pieces, involved an alien with five noses who wouldn't go away. Eventually the narrator offers him a sniff of Dr Rumney's snuff – in all ten nostrils at once – and this has the desired effect.

This short piece was a kind of story, and it paved the way for many more, and eventually for novels, such as *tapestry*, which after twelve years looking for a publisher went on to be shortlisted for the Goldsmiths' Prize. I persisted with novels for many years, before eventually giving up due to my inability to find publishers or agents, and turning to poetry. Poetry I would now see as my natural home – it is less commercial and more open to experiment. It still has an *avant-garde*, something my novelist friends scoff at. Yet my hankering to write novels has never quite gone away, and recently I returned to writing them – I have just finished one called *Invisible Universities*, which reinvents Calvino's *Invisible Cities* and, rather than describing every possible kind of city, describes every possible kind of university, set against a backdrop of strikes, redundancies, wage freezes and closures. Yet as soon as I finished, the old cycle began to repeat itself: I knew that to find a good publisher I had to go through an agent, but when I sent my work to agents, they greeted it, most frequently, with incomprehension: one agent said it wasn't a novel at all, but a 'report', and that they preferred more 'meat and potato' novels. I'm realising for the second time that I cannot write and publish novels in the UK – what I write, for better or worse, is not what the market wants. When I write novels I am wasting my time, I was made to write poems.

And now as I look back on 'A Use for Rumney's' I begin to see it not as a *story* that showed signs that I was going to be a fiction writer, and that that was the path I should follow, but more as a *prose poem*. And as if to underline this, isn't that alien with five noses that won't go away a metaphor for the novelist, the sleuth, always trying to sniff his way to the bottom of the plot? If I'd seen this in the first place I might not have wasted so many years writing novels, I might have turned to poetry straight away, I might have been among Heaney's 'happy men', practising the right art from the start. But at least I'm doing better than Socrates, who only had a few hours to go when he discovered he had been practising the wrong art: I am now giving up novels for good, and dedicating the time I have left to poetry *tout court*.

*

'Always be a poet, even in prose.' (Baudelaire)

*

In her book *No Go the Bogeyman*, pursuing the thread of learning through repetitive lullabys, vocal sounds unattached to meaning, and language learning as 'stored-up play', Marina Warner discusses our aptitude for learning a second language, so much greater in childhood. She points out how Mallarmé, working as an English teacher in Paris, intuited all this when he became fascinated with English nonsense rhymes, which he translated into French for his pupils. A school inspector, she relates, chanced to come in just as Mallarmé was teaching the following rhyme to children of the Lycée Fontanes in 1888:

Lick liar spit
Your tongue shall be slit
And all the dogs in the town
Shall have a little bit.

'The report,' Warner writes, 'was withering: "M. Mallarmé, as he is to remain a teacher of English... should learn English... he should not dictate... foolish rubbish like 'Liar liar lick spit'." He then gave in full, Mallarmé's polished version of the rhyme, and concluded, blustering, "One is tempted to ask oneself if one is not in the presence of a sick man."'

*

In an exhibition on the work of the artist Roger Ackling at the Henry Moore Foundation in Leeds, *Sunlight* – the title refers to Ackling's frequent use of sunlight to burn intricate patterns into driftwood – amongst a display of sketches, objects, plans and notebooks, I came across the following unpublished notebook poem:

```
 |         ||           ||
MY SHOELACE UNDONE
      ||          ||     |       |    ||           /
HUNTING ALONG THE DARKENING HEDGE
   |         ||         |     |
THE TWILIGHT WHITE OWL
  |          ||            ||
MY SHOELACE UNDONE
      ||          ||     |       |    ||
HUNTING ALONG THE DARKENING HEDGE
   |         ||         |     |
THE TWILIGHT WHITE OWL
  |          \            /
MY SHOELACE UNDONE
      ||          ||     |       |    ||           /
HUNTING ALONG THE DARKENING HEDGE
   |         ||         |     |
THE TWILIGHT WHITE OWL
    ||          |          ||
AUTUMN MOON DANCING

ABOVE THE DARKENING HEDGE

THE TWILIGHT WHITE OWL
```

The superscript indicates, in the first two stanzas (identical apart from the variations in the superscript), that Ackling is thinking in terms of syllabics – the stanzas divide into 5/9/5 – perhaps aspiring to a haiku. In the third repeat of the stanza, the superscript is quite different, suggesting a falling and rising voice, indicating that Ackling is thinking in terms of intonation on top of the syllabics. The final stanza, the only one that is markedly different, resolves the syllabic patterning into a traditional haiku (5/7/5). It is unclear to me whether we should read this as a minimalist poem of four stanzas, or notes towards the final stanza, which might stand alone as a haiku. Either way, it is a piece of great beauty and simplicity – you wouldn't publish it like this, but in its notebook form what is striking is the way we get to look over Ackling's shoulder at the process of the writing, the play of word and sense and sound *during* composition, with rare intimacy. It has a lightness, a purity, that takes my breath away – perhaps a lightness which only comes with unpublished work.

*

Reading great poetry for the first time – Rilke, say, or Eliot – I don't understand a word, but I can tell I am in the presence of something greater than me, and it feels exciting, eye-opening, expansive, I am soaring off somewhere – I don't know where – and I love it, and I know already that when I read this again, and again, and again, that while my understanding of it will grow, this strange and completely inexplicable sense of rapture that I am feeling, *now*, as I read it for the first time, will fade.

*

Baudelaire wrote a number of ekphrastic poems over his relatively short writing life, from 'Gypsies Travelling' (after a print by Jacques Callot), to 'Lola de Valence' (after Manet) and 'On *Tasso in Prison* by Eugène Delacroix', but among them all one stands out for its originality of approach, amounting to a new *kind* of ekphrastic poem: 'A Martyr'. It's subtitle – 'Drawing by an unknown master' – hints at the poem's originality, for this is not a poem *after* an existing painting or drawing or print: while it *appears* to describe a work by 'an unknown master', neither the 'drawing' nor the 'master' exists, they are figurations of Baudelaire's painterly imagination. In short, the poem here, rather than following or responding to an *existing* drawing, *is itself* the drawing. As such, the poem has many painterly qualities, appearing to rove over its scene as the eye might rove slowly over a canvas, revealing as it proceeds a room full of sumptuous goods and paintings. It is stuffy, like a hothouse, and in its centre, on a bed, lies the headless corpse of a woman, blood gushing out of it like a stream, as in a painting of a Christian martyrdom. The severed head rests on the night table 'like a ranunculus'. The image is shocking, seemingly gratuitous in its violence, and it is surprising, especially given the poem's hints at necrophilia, that it was *not* among the six poems of *Les Fleurs du Mal* condemned for outrage to public decency in the trial of 1857. On the surface it is a poem of sexual violence and depravity, of precisely the kind that has led to Baudelaire's pigeon-holing as a decadent writer. Yet this is to ignore the painterly dimension of the poem, and if we follow this clue, imagining this is a painting not a poem, its meanings begin to unfold differently. Just as the violence in the background of Delacroix's painting *The Crusaders Entering Constantinople* (1840), much admired by Baudelaire, reflects as much on the French Revolution as it does on the violence of the crusades, so, from another angle, we can see 'A Martyr' as a reflection of a traumatised post-revolutionary sensibility: what else but a guillotine could sever the head of this woman so cleanly? Just as the violently dismembered bodies of an artist such as Louise Bourgeois can be seen as a reflection of millennial dismemberments, so can Baudelaire's severings and disjunctions be seen to reflect the underlying violence of the aftermath of revolution. And here we begin to see the sense in which the 'decadent' of Baudelaire might be not so much about the decadent *in* Baudelaire as about the decadent *around* Baudelaire. And this view is reflected by Nicole Ward Jouve, who comments on Baudelaire's rejection of the word decadence in his defence of Poe: 'A poet,' she writes, 'is not decadent because his work registers the evil and sadness of the world; he would be so only if he revelled in it; and he would be shallow and insensitive if he sang his happiness in the midst of misery. The kind of art he must strive for is one that will exactly record the temper of the times.'

*

Writing on Dryden, like Eliot writing on Milton, Michael Schmidt is able to simultaneously tune in to what is good and what is bad, what opens up and what shuts down. 'If we judge him by the effect he had,' he writes, 'he is great. If we judge the work itself we can't deny him greatness, unless on grounds of limited tonal range (on such grounds Milton himself would fail). Dryden's technical and formal assurance have few parallels. He is a civic, public, social poet. Our age has a distaste for such work and its values, but if we dismiss Dryden, we dismiss the clearest English poet, and the most accomplished of public poets.' It's a powerful defence, but the obverse is perhaps more telling still: 'When Dryden "refined" language, he rid it of dross, but also of much expressive power. He returned his instrument to certain harmonies but it was incapable of some older and deeper strains. The loss is felt not so much in his own work as in the work of his heirs.'

*

Poem on a bench outside Reedham, Norfolk, in memory of Michael Henry James, (1 July 1939 – 14 October 2005):

Here mates sit down, take a rest
You've been out and done your best
Your bag don't look too full today
But it's good that some of them got away
So sit for a while, remember your old pal Mike
I loved these marshes, fell in many a dyke
Did you hear me chuckle when you missed that duck
And say maybe next time you'll have better luck.

The rhyme scheme is conventional heroic couplets, distantly echoing Dryden, though the scansion and music of the poem are unrefined. But the poem's roughness here is its life, and it has life, not least in the twist in the sixth line, where the voice of Mike itself intrudes into the poem, and we realise it is Mike who has been speaking all along. And once we see this we realise too that while most benches that are 'dedicated' are there to memorialise the person – referenced here in 'remember your old pal Mike' – here the bench is actually *for* Mike so that when the first line says 'Here mates sit down', Mike is actually *one* of those mates, and the other mate – the only living one to sit down here – is the person (or poacher?) addressed by Mike's ghost: 'Your bag don't look too full today'. The poem, in brief, while conventional in its appearance, *plays* on the assumptions we make about benches and the people they are there to memorialise. Mike, or the ghostly presence of Mike, *inhabits* the bench, as he *inhabits* the poem.

*

Baudelaire's strange similes are so strange to our eyes, even today, that translators sometimes fail to *see* them and actually substitute something else more conventional *for* them. So, in 'To a Red-Haired Beggar Girl', where Baudelaire imagines the street girl magically transported to a sumptuous boudoir, her would-be suitors, now placed far below her on the social scale, gather outside, awaiting the 'frais déduits' ('deduction'). The phrase is deliberately unpoetic, breaking all rules of poetic decorum, coming as it does not from the language of poetic diction but from the vocabulary of the market, where it refers to a 'deduction of expenses'. The market is relevant to the poem, as it is the dog-eat-dog economy of Second Empire Paris which is the root cause of the wealth gap that is the central subject of the poem, and the disjunction in the *language* of the poem directly reflects this. But it's odd, and remains odd, so in James McGowan's translation, to name only one, the 'frais déduits' are erased, and the would-be suitors who stand in the street 'Spy for the secret sweets / Of your retreat!'

Bibliography

Baudelaire, Charles, *Intimate Journals*, transl. Norman Cameron, with a preface by Richard Howard (London: Penguin, 1995).

Baudelaire, Charles, *The Flowers of Evil*, transl. James McGowan, with an introduction by Jonathan Culler (Oxford: Oxford World's Classics, 1993).

Heaney, Seamus, *The Haw Lantern* (London: Faber, 1987).

Schmidt, Michael, *Lives of the Poets* (London: Weidenfeld & Nicolson, 1998).

Ward Jouve, Nicole, *Baudelaire* (London: Macmillan, 1980).

Warner, Marina, *No Go the Bogeyman* (London: Chatto and Windus, 1998).

Poems

JOHN BIRTWHISTLE

Wateriness

Silvery shock at slight rain skimming the pond.
A rainbow mirrored in water of forest-green.

Water is essential to life. Without water
we would not have all these paintings of water.

Philosophy

My daughter studies a famous paper
What is it Like to Be a Bat?

while I am wondering
what it's like to be my daughter.

Cutting

The disused cutting reverts to
        a cliff-edge of limestone.
To every crevice its secret
        mosses, its redlegged cranesbill.
A chinking within the wall is
        betraying the nest of a wagtail.
The railway has been and gone. Just
        think of the navvies; think of the Irish.

To One about To Emigrate

When two hundred years ago one left the shore
of Ireland for a new life, the family would hold
an American Wake and say their last farewells
expecting to see each other never again in this world.

The whole townland watched the disappearing ship.
They followed it out to the furthest tip of rock.
Nightfall, and bonfires would send a very last word.
There was even dancing.
                                        But what need
separate us nowadays from the elegant girl
who swirled us children round and round in the garden
until we were silly with laughter? She is as near

as the screen. And so we accompany you
as you strike out afresh and we keep in touch.

Description in Winter

Scarcely mirrored in the ditch
a lemon pip of a sun

yet the field takes place.

Grass in the shadow of a hedge
brittle with frost;
in the open, spangled with dew.

Hard to believe a crop
already nailed in the ground.

Rush Hour, 24th April 2024

Five cavalry horses throw off their riders
and gallop gallop through rush hour traffic

in central London, four of them black and one
a superbly white horse drenched in blood

while our surrealist poet is just waking up
to write down his dreams before he forgets

On Reading of Ghetto Deportation

She closed the book and stared into the fire:

Lorries idling
    fumes wasted on the air

        For reasons of hygiene your children
        are being taken where they will suffer
        no hunger or sickness any more.

Hastily scribbled names
    pinned to childish lapels

        BLESS YOU GOOD PEOPLE FOR LOOKING
        AFTER MY LITTLE BOY HE IS POORLY HIS
        BOTTOM COMES OUT HIS NAME IS ABRAHAM

It is possible to love the dead.

Nineteen Years

J. KATES

'Rip van Winkle' is the story of a man who fell into an enchanted sleep and woke up twenty years later to a world transformed by a revolution. In 1984, I looked out the window of the Admiral Benbow Inn in downtown Jackson, Mississippi, and watched as an integrated group of businessmen entered the hotel for what looked to be a working power breakfast. It was my first return to Mississippi since 1965, when I had returned home from working in 1964's 'Freedom Summer' campaign for voter registration and Black empowerment and its aftermath. I felt like Rip van Winkle. During my two-decade-long sleep a revolution had occurred, and now I had awakened into that new world.

The motivating purpose of coming back to Mississippi was to research a novel I was trying to write, one that used many of my experiences in 1964 and 1965. I wanted to catch the emotions and ambiguities of that time, emotions and ambiguities I had never included in my original letters north, partly because those were crafted as conscious propaganda for the Movement, but also because I was not capable then of putting my own complexities into prose.

In deeper fact, I was trying to reclaim that experience through fiction, writing that set me to external as well as internal research. The fiction drew heavily on memory, memory so unconscious but still so vivid that it served surprisingly accurate as a roadmap when I returned to the landscape of the northern Delta. Driving south from Memphis in a rented car, I stopped on the shoulder of one road and let myself recreate the roads of two decades before, only to realise that I had already mapped that route in the draft of one of my chapters. But it was the external research that impelled me to return. I wanted to confirm and revitalise memories I was folding into fiction. In Panola County, I stopped in Como to look around the town and eat a meal in the one Black café, took a side trip to visit the family who had housed me there in 1964 but who had since moved to another county, stayed for a couple of nights in Batesville, and then drove south to Jackson, where I passed one full day in front of a microfiche reader in the library reading the *Clarion-Ledger* for the whole summer to recapture flavours and atmospheres, weather and daily life. These readings underlined the changes twenty years had wrought. So did the back stories I learned from those I visited, long lost hosts and new acquaintances.

The day I returned to Natchez was comic. While everyone in Panola County had remembered me, I did not expect anyone in the southwestern city to do so. So there I was, a strange white man in a rental car driving through the streets of Black Natchez, stopping people practically at random to ask for particular residents by name. I knew it would take a long time before I found someone who knew me, someone who could vouch for me from their own memory. Before that, a person I had been asking for might have been in the next room, but no one was going to let me know.

Finally, I found Jessie Bernard, who had run the NAACP office in 1965, and through her learned about others I had known and worked with. But it was a superficial, touristic return, very different from the continuing embrace of Panola County.

*

Ten years before my return, in June 1974, a federal judge had ruled that Boston schools were *de facto*, even if not *de jure*, segregated, and he ordered the city to implement a controversial programme of interschool bussing. This unleashed a violent backlash of white community rancour which continued all fall. In response, local civil-rights organizations called for a March Against Racism on 14 December, with one of the slogans reading 'Little Rock 1957 / Selma 1965 / Boston 1974'.

At that time, I was teaching high school in Wayland, an affluent Boston suburb. My students were a decade younger than I was. I had told them very little about my freedom work. In a way, even though I had stayed active in social causes through a year in graduate school and a war in southeast Asia, I thought I had put Mississippi behind me. Why? It's a question I later took up with the Student Nonviolent Co-ordinating Committee veteran Jimmie Travis, who also regretted years lost before we began weaving our stories into our ongoing lives. For years also, Jimmie and I were out of direct touch, although he would occasionally call my mother late at night and pour out his heart to her. The reasons were different for him and for me. Many of the SNCC staff people had burned out, suffering from what we now label post-traumatic stress syndrome, and they reacted in various ways, almost all of which involved recoiling one way or another from the immediate past. Jimmie could tell his own story of a transformative trip to Africa and what followed. The Veterans of the Civil Rights Movement.

For volunteers like me, it was complicated in a different way. Mississippi had taught us not to thrust ourselves forward as leaders, but to put our skills to use to create self-sustaining communities. So we did not strip our arms and show our scars as we engaged in the rising feminist, anti-war, Chicano, gay and other movements, even as we contributed to them both as ordinary participants and as leaders. It would have been bad form, and possibly counter-productive. We had learned to lead from behind, and we continued to do so. We distrusted the strutters, but there were few enough of those. We passed into grown-up lives as organisers, academics, teachers. The roster of leaders of the movements of the 1960s and 1970s who originally came out of the Mississippi Summer Project, from Mario Savio to Susan Brownmiller, is too large to list.

And there were deeper psychological reasons. Our guilt ran deep. No matter what our reason told us, we knew that we had left Mississippi for the relative safety of our own communities, while the people we had worked so closely with and, in some cases, had led into vulnerable positions, did not have our choice to walk away. Through 1964 and 1965 and later, churches and community centres continued to be burned. People were killed. Vernon Dahmer died defending his burning house in 1966. Wharlest Jackson was blown up in his pick-up truck in Natchez in 1967. I finished college with honours that year. I taught school in one affluent, mostly white suburb, then another, and another. I married and moved to the suburbs myself. I divorced.

The night of 13 December 1974, I dreamed I was back in Panola County, all of us sitting around an abundant welcome table at the Batesville Sundry general store and café run by Mr. and Mrs. Thomas, where we used to celebrate every small victory in the summer of 1964. The conversation was loud and convivial. It was a reunion, volunteers and local people together. But there was one person I couldn't see, the farmer in whose house I had stayed when I worked in Batesville. I looked all around the table.

'Where's Mr. Charlie Johnson?' I asked.

Stunned silence, then finally someone said, 'He's sitting right next to you'.

I woke up crying.

On the morning of the 14th, *The Boston Globe* published a Doonesbury comic strip, a Walden College reunion. In the second panel, Megaphone Mark asks, 'Do you remember when we used to have the courage of our convictions?' Michael Doonesbury asks, 'Do you remember when we thought we could make a difference?' 'Do you remember how we once cared?' 'Do you remember how we once gave a damn?'

I joined the march.

*

When I finally did return to Panola County in 1984, I was welcomed unreservedly by those we had worked with before. We didn't gather at the Thomas Sundry, which had long since drifted into neglect, but at a community centre that had refused to let us hold mass meetings there during Freedom Summer. Robert and Mona Miles, the couple who had encouraged, anchored and sustained our Panola County project in 1964, fêted my coming as if I had been their own prodigal son. They peppered me with questions about my own life in New Hampshire. They tasted tentatively my house gift of maple syrup and frankly stated that they preferred their own sorghum molasses with morning grits. By this time, they were honoured citizens of the county. Mr. Miles, a man the whites had once tried to run out of town with firebombs and rifle shots – his house still marked with the bullet holes – was now the elder statesman of local politics. No one could expect to win an election without his endorsement. The local weekly newspaper ran a four-part series telling their heroic story.

'Look,' Mr. Miles told me, 'we have a McDonald's in Batesville now. That wouldn't have been possible without integration'

I sighed inwardly. We had worked for the Beloved Community, and we had been rewarded with McDonald's. But for the Miles's and the others of Panola County, this was victory. Mississippi was America. They remained grateful for our help. And every Christmas thereafter until she died in 1992, Mrs. Miles sent me a box of pecans from the tree beside their house. There was no reason or room for my guilt in their understanding.

That first return, though, Mr. Miles had a request. He had his own list of all the volunteers in the Batesville project, and he wanted me to try to get in touch with them. I promised to do my best. We had indeed scattered, and I had not kept up connections with anyone else from the Batesville project, but I tried to keep my promise. My first success was to track down a volunteer who had since become a professor of mathematics at a Southern university. I dialled his office telephone number and he answered.

The instant he learned who I was and why I was calling, he burst out in one anguished gust of words, 'I didn't mean to leave early. I had to go. My grandmother had died!' In his distress I heard a magnified outcry of my own feelings. For two decades, he had carried his sense of abandoning all too close to the surface, and I was accidentally the scratch that opened his wound.

In the end, even after having published a couple of chapters, I set the fiction aside. It wasn't the story I had to tell. 'The past is never dead. It's not even past', William Faulkner famously wrote. Mississippi.

In the Beginning: A New Translation of the *Enuma Elish*

Johannes Haubold, Sophus Helle, Enrique Jiménez and Selena Wisnom (eds.), *Enuma Elish: The Babylonian Epic of Creation* (Bloomsbury) £75

Reviewed by James Dowthwaite

How did the world begin? The Babylonians answered this question with an explanation expedient for a nascent empire: it was the work of their city god, Marduk. In the beginning the gods of fresh water, *Apsû* and sea water, *Tiamat*, mixed their waters together and fathered the first gods. These gods, however, were too noisy for Apsû, who wanted to destroy them. Ea, the wisest of the gods, got wind of Apsû's plan and killed him, fathering a son, Marduk, on Apsû's corpse, with his consort. Tiamat is eventually convinced to take revenge and the gods elect Marduk as their champion. He eventually defeats Tiamat and creates the world out of her body. The poem that told of this story was central to Babylonian cosmology and identity, as well as a fundamental part of the ritual of the *Akitu*, the New Year Festival – the most important date in Babylon's calendar. Here it was read to a sacred statue of Marduk himself.

While *Gilgamesh* has been well-mined for its wealth of poetic material, the *Enuma Elish* is much less known. It is this that a new translation by Sophus Helle, accompanied by interpretations and contextualising essays by experts in the field, attempts to rectify. The work is the first in Bloomsbury's new series, *The Library of Babylonian Literature*. The contributors, and above all, the editors, are to be praised for this considerable archaeological achievement. There have been versions of the *Enuma Elish* in English before (most notably by W.G. Lambert and by Stephanie Dalley), but the editors have brought this material together under new perspectives and in new ways to offer it to a wider literary public.

It has proven immensely difficult to make Akkadian verse sing as beautifully as it does in the original. The poetic conventions are far from our own standards of taste. The prosody is rhythmical but not strictly metrical, with an average of four heavily stressed syllables per line, often with a caesura between; there is much alliteration, word play and chiasmus, perhaps comparable to the Hebrew Psalms. The verse is musical, with heavy use of repetitions and parallelisms – forms that are largely eschewed in modern English. Thus, translators are faced with a series of difficult choices on whether to maintain very foreign idioms or to look for distant modern equivalents; fidelity and readability, as something recognisably modern, are sometimes at strife. All of these considerations are to say nothing of the aesthetic task of making it sing.

Helle thus had an unenviable task of balancing music and philology. At times the one element predominates over the other, and perhaps the poet demands more license and liberty with aesthetic departures than the scholar, but on the whole, the material shines in a way that maintains Akkadian images in English style. Consider the following lines, in which Marduk surveys Tiamat's body and begins to create the earth: 'The Lord grew calm and examined her corpse / To carve up the watery mass and create artful things'. Helle preserves the image but renders it forensically modern. The importance of this approach cannot be understated, as it announces the broader wealth of Akkadian literature to audiences whose primary interest is new music.

The essays present the *Enuma Elish* as a portal to further encounter with Akkadian cultures, as intended by the editors of this new series, and their contributions show this well. Enrique Jiménez provides the historical background of the poem's composition; Johannes Haubold relates it beautifully to ideas of poetry as divine communication; Selena Wisnom, an accomplished playwright and poet on Akkadian themes in her own right, considers the poem as a rich web of references to other, even older literary works, both Akkadian and Sumerian; and Helle himself examines the poem's enduring questions of form.

Fittingly for a poem about our origins, this volume opens us to new poetic departures.

Scissoring Men out of the Picture

Hilary Holladay, *The Power of Adrienne Rich: A Biography* (Princeton University Press) £20

Reviewed by Gregory Woods

Adrienne Rich's career began with patriarchal endorsement. While she was still a student, W.H. Auden picked her first collection, *A Change of World*, for the Yale Series of Younger Poets. Yet his introduction to it did not mention Rich until the seventh of ten paragraphs, and when it did he called her poems 'neatly and modestly dressed'. At Harvard she studied under F.O. Matthiessen, he of *American Renaissance*, who would later add her to *The Oxford Book of American Verse*. Since then, she has had a secure place in anthologies both canonical and anti-canonical. Collections of US lesbian verse have relied on her tutelary presence.

A poetry syllabus Rich herself taught at Columbia in 1967 included no women. In retrospect, as Hilary Holladay notes, this 'shows how far and fast she would have to travel in the next several years to become one of the nation's premiere feminists'. Purely in terms of gender and sexuality, the distance she travelled was enormous – and she didn't take the pretty route.

Rich later conceded that, in her first two collections, she had been blocking 'with assimilation and technique' the development of her own poetic voice: she had, in effect, been trying to write as a man, or at least to a male standard; and that is before we even begin to consider her growth as a woman who was lesbian. Early on, it was routine, if painful, to re-gender pronouns for universalising effect. Even so, Holladay rightly calls the circumspect early poem 'Stepping Backward' 'A beautiful, brainy love poem with Sapphic fingerprints all over it'.

Looking back, Rich said: 'I had been looking for the Women's Liberation movement since the 1950s. I came into it in 1970.' She had married in 1953 to get away from her own family, and bore three sons. In 1970, that key year, her husband committed suicide. About four years later she began her first affair with a woman, and another year later she came out publicly as lesbian. Separatism and free verse would develop in lockstep. Of course, when she began to concentrate on her experience as a woman, she was criticised for becoming too personal.

According to Holladay, 'Rich wrote some of the best poems of her career while she was in limbo between her past as a married heterosexual woman and her future as a partnered lesbian'. She is referring to some of the work in *Diving into the Wreck* (1973), moving on from poems addressing 'the raw pain of her life as a heterosexual woman' to others in which she 'scissored men out of the picture'. With all the zeal of the recent convert, having become a radical, lesbian feminist Rich avoided contact with men, insisting on negotiating her contract at Brandeis University with a woman rather than with the department's male chair. At a major reading in 1975, she refused to take questions from male students. Even her connections with other feminist women were tightly selective: we are told she was not interested in developing friendships with straight women such as Elaine Showalter. In the early 1970s, probably by way of Virginia Woolf, she developed an interest in androgyny to 'relieve each sex of its burden of being all to the other' ('I am the androgyne', she says in 'The Stranger', and 'I am she: I am he' in 'Diving into the Wreck'). However, at a reading in the Library of Congress in April 1981, she stated firmly: 'I write as a woman, as a lesbian, and as a feminist. I make no claim to be universal, neuter, or androgynous.'

Rich disapproved of gay men's sexist responses to the anti-gay rights activist Anita Bryant, and refused to write a blurb for Karla Jay and Allen Young's essay collection *Out of the Closets* (1978), reluctant to endorse comparisons between lesbians and gay men. Yet she later allowed her poems to be included in such defining anthologies as *The Penguin Book of Homosexual Verse* (1983) and Carl Morse and Joan Larkin's *Gay and Lesbian Poetry in Our Time* (1988); and there was something of a rapprochement with gay men during the worst years of the AIDS epidemic.

Holladay reveals that the addressee of the renowned 'Twenty-One Love Poems' was her therapist Lilly Engler, an ex of Susan Sontag's. Rich was writing these poems and *Of Woman Born*, her excellent study of motherhood, while in a relationship with Engler. The subsequent partnership with Michelle Cliff, originally her copyeditor, lasted for the remaining thirty-six years of Rich's life, when the poet was increasingly tortured by rheumatoid arthritis.

A rather dry, austere figure emerges from this narrative, notwithstanding Holladay's attempts to humanise her. There is great tenderness in many of the poems, but you can't help noticing that her biography has just two indexed page references for 'relationship with sons'.

Making Strange

Mark Ford, *A Guest Among Stars: Essays on Twentieth-Century Poets* (The Black Spring Press Group) £20.00

Reviewed by Sunil Iyengar

In Mark Ford's fourth collection of essays, the subjects include pre-modern, modern and postmodern poets whose lives and works have been treated exhaustively by prior critics and biographers. But for those who have encountered his pieces in the *London Review of Books* and the *New York Review of Books* (from which all but two of these entries are drawn), or who have enjoyed his *LRB* podcast with Seamus Perry, or who have admired his two critical biographies of Thomas Hardy, it will come as no surprise that Ford finds new approaches to well-examined figures including Housman, Eliot, Pound, Larkin, Gunn and Hughes. What continues to animate a reader is Ford's 'walking possession' of the poets he considers.

The phrase is attributed to Ian Hamilton, and its legal provenance is apt: Ford discriminates nicely in his selection of quotes, and in his appraisals of individual poems or careers he renders justice without equivocation. His rebukes are relative sparseness: Ford's persona throughout these essays is of an intrepid voyager who, while he may go in for a little stargazing, is not too besotted to explain his enthusiasms to a newcomer.

The book's title comes from lines by Douglas Crase, the sole living poet to whom he devotes an essay:

> it is
> You who are rising above them and you are not there.
> Like a rocket in winter, I have been there to see you
> Logged in as a guest among stars – only you,
> Though you're lovely to look at, expensive to own,
> And though in demand without letup, you are not there.

Introducing this passage, Ford likens Crase to Ashbery and praises, in both cases, a 'mysterious fusion of overpowering fascination with complete disconnection that attends our most potent artistic experiences'. And yet the sensibility behind these pages is far from anonymous. A poetics of disjunction – expressed so vividly by his reverence for Ashbery (a cache of letters between the poets first appeared in *PN Review* and closes this volume) – qualifies Ford's criteria as a critic.

He also prizes poets who exhibit 'curiosity and élan' – Apollinaire for example, subject of another essay. It turns out that Ford began corresponding with Ashbery while researching Raymond Roussel, who inspired the French surrealists and later, like Apollinaire, the New York School. He thus celebrates the avant-gardism that linked certain French and American poets. Apollinaire's 'long poems, like those of Whitman and O'Hara, seem to expand and prolong themselves as effortlessly as amoeba in a petri dish, [and] beneath the shifting decors and personae a sense of genuine perplexity often emerges', Ford writes. He enumerates the French poet's American poet-translators. By the end of the essay, we are at Frank O'Hara's 1966 funeral, where the painter Philip Gustafson said O'Hara 'was our Apollinaire'.

Ford seizes on the virtue of 'genuine perplexity' – a diffidence or circuitousness that thwarts direct communication and complete knowledge – in promoting the works of other writers he is keen to advance. Of a poem by Walter de le Mare in homage to Edward Thomas ('To E.T.: 1917'), he locates a 'familiar de la Marean equilibrium of obliquely imagined exchange, like that between Traveller and Listeners', the titles of two of his most famous poems, 'an equilibrium that is wholly at odds with the death-drive so in evidence in late Thomas poems'. In A.R. Ammons, he finds 'an expansive series of free-flowing songs of the self pursued into whatever byways or loops of inquiry his consciousness happened to wander'. But candour does not mean closure. According to Ford, 'the "de-denominated" divinity of Ammons's world is entropy, and its chief signifier the colon, which was relentlessly used by the poet in almost all phases of his career as a means of linking the disparate but coexisting, and so staving off completion.'

At times 'genuine perplexity' is manifest in Ford's reactions as a practical literary critic, as with the steel trap of Eliot's annotated poems, in two volumes edited by Christopher Ricks and Jim McCue. 'But what exactly is the difference in reading such notes,' he asks, 'between an interesting allusion or echo and a mere verbal coincidence?' Surveying the Epilogue of Ted Hughes's bizarre *Gaudete* (1977), Ford wonders at 'how little vatic indeterminacy suited Hughes's particular poetic gifts'. He is blunter in describing a passage from Derek Walcott's *The Prodigal* (2004): 'One marvels at the skill to pull off such a feat of rhetoric – without really wanting to read a lot more of it'.

Of the fourteen essays here, three centre on women writers: Joan Murray, whom Auden awarded the Yale Younger Poets prize, posthumously, and about whose archives Ford furnishes a personal anecdote; Adrienne Rich, whose work, he writes, is 'an intermeshing of poetry and history more extensive and searching than that to be found in any of her contemporaries' – an arresting claim; and Joni Mitchell. 'I am on a lonely road and I am traveling / Traveling, traveling, traveling / Looking for something, what can it be?' she sang in 'All I Want' on her album *Blue* (1971). As a fellow traveller, one who exemplifies the same 'openness to contingency' he also ascribes to Ammons, Ford might say the same.

All of nature laughs together

Nikolai Zabolotsky, *Columns* (1929, translated by Dmitri Manin, Arc, 2023) £11.99

Reviewed by Fred Warren

No matter how many Euro 2025 matches you sat through, it's unlikely you would have heard the beautiful game described in the manner of Nikolai Zabolotsky's 1927 poem 'Football'. Shifting to the ball's perspective, Zabolotsky's mock-heroic verses describe how the whirling orb 'apprehends the iron bane of boots'; how it:

> steams, puffs out, cackles with spite,
> [...]
> And racks the forward with a fight

The poem ends with the forward lying in a hospital, the image of the infernal ball hovering above them. Interestingly, FIFA estimates that the average footballer spends just 1 minute and 49 seconds of a game in possession of the ball. The rest of the game, as Zabolotsky's poem suggests, is really just an elaborate (and dangerous) dance around an object forever beyond control.

With its vertiginous shifts in subject and geography, 'Football' is a good starting place for navigating Zabolotsky's short collection *Columns* (*Stolbtsy*), first published in 1929 and newly translated by Dmitri Manin. Born outside Kazan in 1903, Zabolotsky came of age in the harsh yet artistically fertile climate of 1920s Leningrad (St Petersburg) and belonged to the short-lived, avant-garde group OBERIU (Association for Real Art). A glance at *Columns,* then, might suggest a cerebral book of modernist poetry aiming to capture the metropolis and its mental life; of blurry apparitions and metro stations. But responding to a city still thick with the memory of revolution, famine and civil war, Zabolotsky gives us something far headier: a series of visceral vignettes where decaying limbs, rivers, animals, Red Army sentinels and boozy vapours jostle for prominence.

Food is everywhere in these poems; in 'The Bakery', a herculean struggle ensues in the early hours as a loaf is triumphantly born, while in 'At the Fishmonger's' the narrator salivates over a sturgeon 'blushing like a virgin'. The food often ends up assuming a sacredness, betraying the experience of a poet who, as a student, allegedly survived on black bread and boiled water, a temporary bout of scurvy notwithstanding. Such hardships make the poet's anger at the bourgeoise consumption associated with the New Economic Policy of the 1920s (which saw the Soviet government permit the partial reintroduction of private enterprise) all the sharper, as in 'A Wedding' when he lampoons 'a bulging flock of fleshy dames':

> Their breath coarse with unsated passions,
> They munch on glutinous confections,
> They let their guts loose from the laces

Even here, though, the focus on the breath and sheer corporeality of the women can't help but turn this satire into something far more grounded and sensual.

This preoccupation with the fleshiness of life is not just designed to shock and can be seen as part of Zabolotsky's broader philosophical concern with life beyond the human. This is developed more fully in the second part of *Columns*, which moves beyond the city walls to the rural environs of Zabolotsky's youth. In 'A Walk', his sympathies turn to the 'nameless' domestic animals, their 'toils untold, unnoticed tortures', while the brilliant 'Here in Our Dwellings' depicts onlookers struggling to comprehend the temporality and 'dewy breathing' of trees, before finding their own bodies caught in the process of decay:

> The waves of wetness course within our legs.
> And now the moisture streaming upwards races
> To wash and refresh our leafy faces

The son of an agronomist, Zabolotsky wrote verse that expresses a care for the living world without ever shirking from the messy, violent realities of decomposition and nutrient recycling needed for its continuation.

Zabolotsky's own artistic evolution was cut short when he was imprisoned and exiled in 1938 (he would die, his reputation partially rehabilitated, in 1958). His unique blend of body horror, childish babble and pastoral utopia, however, remains as striking today as ever. These inventive and accessible translations from Manin will, it is to be hoped, allow new readers to start discovering his work – the act of translation particularly befitting the work of a poet so concerned with detailing the ever-changing forms of nature, whether that be the thought of a hungry poet or the shape of a plodding bull.

Mourning Doves

Karen Solie, *Wellwater* (Picador) £12.99

Reviewed by Diana Leca

Karen Solie's latest poetry collection, *Wellwater*, is full of unheralded life forms that survive even our grisliest eradication attempts: 'foxtail, cleavers, sow thistle, kochia'. 'The Climbing Vine', one of the most striking poems in the collection, tells of a creeping plant that emerges suddenly and, troublingly, will not go away: 'arm over arm in its wet clothes', the vine 'hauled itself to the second-floor balcony' and 'spread out'. In an interview with the *LARB*, Solie spoke of her preferred formal structures ('stanzas of regular lengths, sonnet-like poems'), confessing: 'I have a real need for symmetry'. But 'The Climbing Vine' is not left-justified, and there are bits of text scattered across the page like plant cuttings borne by the wind. While this works to slow the line, the creeping plant stubbornly advances. Had it been permitted its monstrous growth, the vine, with all the gumption of Milton's Satan – '[w]ould have torn the house down and stood on the ruin / tossing its hook at the downspout of Heaven'. You can't help but cheer for it.

Several poems in *Wellwater* are like this: they look to disquieting, compromised forms of life for lessons about how to persist in a time of climactic ruin. I hesitate to use this word, 'lessons', because Solie is not a moralising poet. Neither are her poems' conclusions about how to live very clear, and certainly not very instructive. Instead, they are full of beclouded vision: fog, mist, wildfire smoke, freezing rain, dust. At times, too, the syntax twists itself into unfamiliar terrain and readers must climb back up line by line to make their meaning.

A sonneteer by training, Solie often slips in a volta-like jolt. Here is a bit from 'Smoke':

> Disabused of an illusion, we say the fog has lifted,
> the smoke has cleared, the dust
> has settled, and now we see,
>
> though what arises is not clarity
> but a set of new misgivings

Wellwater's poems churn like this, tumbling into minuscule moments of insight – or, at least, insights into the depths of befuddlement. The comfort of clarity (along with the comfort of rhyme, which is hinted at in *see / clarity*) is denied over and over. Denied, too, is the sense that more knowledge or truth about the world's ruin is required to rescue it. In 'Just Say the Word', this is made explicit: 'I have only ever wanted to see things as they are. Until I did, / And experience narrowed to a fact impossible to turn around in.' The sense of being squeezed in is strong in the collection, with its rat traps and windowless 'micro-suites'. Some of the poems are like this, too. The third section of 'Parable of the Rat', for instance, is composed as a snug sonnet with short lines and a series of negatives that act like the dead ends of a maze. In *Wellwater*, no one is able to flee: mourning doves 'rise and are killed and rise / and are killed'. Unable to leap, pronghorn antelope 'must scrabble under' fences, 'tearing their cloaks on the barbs'. The reader's experience is not far removed.

There is a single word in Immanuel Kant's *Anthropology from a Pragmatic Point of View* that fits Solie's work like a key in a lock: the 'startling' (*das Auffallende*). Unlike pure fright, which scrambles the mind, Kant argues that being startled acts as a 'stimulus to astonishment'. '[I]t is proper for art,' he wrote in 1798, 'to represent the usual from a point of view that will make it startling', a fitting description of – if not Solie's task – then her accomplishment.

But is it beautiful? Poems like 'Red Spring' are heavy on fact ('the infant snub-nosed coleoptile / climbs from the cradle of the GMO seed patent, / the earliest stage at which herbicides // may be applied'). They also include agricultural chemical brand-names ('Buctril M™'; 'Luxxur™ for problematic grass weeds'), pushing against out-loud readability. 'I'm sorry, I can't make this beautiful', the poet admits towards the end of the poem. No apology is needed; out of such unwieldy material, Solie shapes her verse and its spooky loveliness. As herbicides are laid down around them, 'white-tailed fawns sleep inside wild chokecherry / in hollowed-out rooms a man can stand up in'.

'Red Spring', along with three other poems, was composed for the *Project Earth: Green Chapter*, a collaborative performance Solie undertook with several Canadian musicians – a response through art to the wreckage of the planet. Although Solie was the sole poet, it's not hard to imagine her voice starring alongside chamber music. Intensely cerebral, her poems nevertheless bear a distinct musicality, with her lines often drawn into metrical regularity ('Is this beauty, all this grass?').

If you put your ear to a poem like 'The Grasslands', you might hear all the little noises living in her lines, especially the clicks and clacks: 'wild liquorice, clover, corn mint'; 'Quicksand and sinkholes of the Killdeer Badlands'. The clamorous */k/* sound is made by pushing a small gust of air through the back of your throat; it moves noisily through Solie's descriptions of the 'kingdom of grass': *cut-leaf, procumbent, long-bracted, creeping, panicled, common.*

Wellwater ask us to listen to delicate noises:

> In winter you might hear
> an elderly grass blade
> shrugging off a shawl of frost

Or, perhaps, 'a vole clearing her throat'. Listening to the barely audible takes on an urgency in Solie's work. 'Be quiet for once', the poem tells us, and something in the verse, or grassy verge, might startle us awake.

Any country in the world

Krisztina Tóth, *My Secret Life* (Bloodaxe Books) £12

Reviewed by Nóra Blascsók

Considering the fact that around two million people from that part of the world call the UK their home, Eastern European voices are shockingly underrepresented in UK literature, especially poetry. Those reading translated literature might already be familiar with Hungarian novelists such as International Booker Prize winning László Krasznahorkai, Nobel Prize winning Imre Kertész and PEN Translation Prize winning Magda Szabó, but books of Hungarian poetry in translation are few and far between, and awareness of them is even lower.

Krisztina Tóth is one of the most important Hungarian poets of her generation, but this is the first book of her poetry in English, translated by the eminent Budapest-born English poet and translator George Szirtes. The work in this book has been selected by Tóth from five of her collections, published over a twenty-year period (2001–21), as well as including some of her previously uncollected poems.

It is easy enough to read her work as the product of socioeconomic circumstances. It is after all what most British readers will associate with Hungary: post-communist economic crisis, disillusionment and poverty. Tóth is part of the generation of writers who came of age in 1989, and the melancholy permeating these poems is undeniable. However, as Szirtes highlights, there is so much more to these poems dealing with universal themes such as love, desire, loss, ageing and mortality. To a fellow Hungarian who grew up in 1980s/90s Budapest, but then emigrated to the UK in the 2000s, this, above all, is a feminist book.

An English friend who accidentally picked the book up off my couch and turned straight to 'Ode to Men of Fifty' felt compelled to read some of the lines aloud, smiling. 'I checked the size of my ass / in the mirror, and well, it's not what it was, / yet I fervently desire you' are words that will resonate with female readers of a certain age everywhere. Her poems are conversational and informal, many of them addressing us readers like friends. She uses irony and tongue-in-cheek humour in places and ways that English-speaking poets perhaps would not. The irony and humour often mask something sinister under the surface, like in the poem 'Gumtree', where a woman almost buys a blow-up doll for her child by accident. Despite the humour ('so it would have a daddy') this is a dark and menacing poem portraying something (sadly) universal ('outbid by someone / who wanted a little girl with a terrified face'). The same theme reappears in 'Valley Road', where a woman goes running with two stones and we all suspect the dogs following her are of the male, human kind. This sinister undertone to Tóth's poems becomes especially poignant once you find out her story as a writer living in exile after receiving death threats in Hungary for daring to suggest the inclusion of more contemporary female writers on the school curriculum.

The female body takes centre stage in this book, and it is a body that goes through transformation: the body that desires ('But I could still not help wanting you wrapped / about me at night'), the body that has given birth ('There's a faint scar where my son pushed his way out'), the aging body ('I don't know what to make of the widening of my hips') and the body that is eventually '*released from the prison of this world of vanities*'.

The first poem, 'East European Triptych', is the only one dealing explicitly with 'Eastern European-ness' (perhaps a deliberate choice), but there will be something UK readers find essentially (and unexpectedly) relatable in these poems of disillusionment and melancholy. Reading lines such as 'My mouth full of amalgam fillings, / my heart full of inherited anxieties' or 'my veins are full of circulating poisons', they will be faced with the uncomfortable reality that late-stage capitalist UK is not so different from post-communist Eastern Europe after all.

This collection is another reminder that 'accessible' does not mean 'easy' or lacking depth. Tóth's language might be conversational and informal, but her poems often serve up surprising changes of tone (i.e. in 'Send me a smile' 'Before it hardens a chestnut is a leaf on a tree' to 'Crazy, I say, to think I'm one of nature's nerds'). I found her poems lingering in my mind long after reading. She is a master of the unsaid.

Riveted

Jamie McKendrick, *Drypoint* (Faber) £10.99

Reviewed by Andrew Wynn Owen

I remember the moment I was first riveted by a McKendrick poem, one winter morning flicking through the *London Review of Books*: 'We that have been hunting all the day / are mighty tired, our hair is dank with sweat / and by our hunting helmets plastered flat'. That poem, which rolls on magnificently, calls to the reader from a misty, historical world very unlike ours, while carrying in its voice great and deep emotion, an emotion that is still ours to access and one which, in our better moments, we do access. I was riveted, as I say. By 'riveted', I mean to mark out the experience of being struck by a poem as if by a thunderbolt, not understanding how it does what it does and wanting to understand.

Chronicler of contemporary British life Lamorna Ash writes, 'What I do not understand I have always been drawn towards' (*Don't Forget We're Here Forever*, Bloomsbury). Aristotle observed a similar phenomenon: 'It is through wonder that men now begin and originally began to philosophize; wondering in the first place at obvious perplexities, and then by gradual progression raising questions about the greater matters too, e.g. about the changes of the moon and of the sun, about the stars and about the origin of the universe' (*Metaphysics*). It is that which remains at least somewhat elusive to our faculty of understanding that draws us in. Quite a lot of artworks are relatively boring (i.e. not wonder-inducing), once one is an adult with some degree of specialization in the relevant medium, because they are encompassed by one's faculty of understanding and therefore predictable in at least one of the respects that most matter aesthetically. But McKendrick's poem stood out from the page. It eluded me. I did not have the foggiest idea how he had done it. Why does the hunting metaphor work so well there? What on Earth (or elsewhere) is the poet talking about? Try as I might, I cannot dissolve it in the hydrochloric acid of analysis. It is golden and only some technique of alchemy, the application of an *aqua regia* that is not currently to hand, will break it down. One part of me does not want to break it down, while another part does. Such are the contradictory desires incited by artworks that are elusive in this way.

McKendrick is elusive in this fine way in *Drypoint* too, a decade later, making eloquent sense while pointing towards sites of wonder. There is an opening suite based around the gifts of the magi, carried off with jovial panache: 'Nugget' sees McKendrick, in pandemic lockdown, 'sitting through / "Aussie Gold-Diggers" [a mis-remembrance of the television programme "Aussie Gold Hunters"?]'. There is a set of Edenic poems, mixed with Dantescan reflections, supported by the beautiful translation 'Green Angels'. This translation is something of a centrepiece for the book, spotlighting the guardian angels of purgatory, those 'heavenly hawks' in green raiment. The final section contains a fantastical and uplifting poem called 'The Lion-Tree', which concerns a mythical tree mentioned by Pliny the Elder, from which the Argo was said to have been made. This poem somehow manages to be uplifting, against the grain of the downbeat propositional content of its final lines: 'Perhaps it was the furious winds that finished it or else / the tree at last grew tired of existence'. The closing clash between undaunted uplift and speculative sigh is perhaps the main component of what makes this poem another of McKendrick's elusive successes.

In many of these poems, an enabling condition for the elusiveness is deft and somewhat understated patterning. In a piece beginning 'In her last week lying without words' (a section of a sequence called 'Inheritance'), McKendrick presents a short family tale that ends with ruminations about how to dispose of an old service revolver. Here the work resembles Muldoon in form (half-rhyming, line-length-switching), but is McKendrick's own characterful and likeable fare in terms of content: historical, unassuming, wry and resilient. Elsewhere, the formal touches resemble those of John Fuller: in 'Lunar Vista', McKendrick rhymes 'survey' and 'scurvy' – a playful, nearly anagrammatic rhyming pair, which recalls Fuller's recent forays into anagrammatic rhyme – e.g. in a lovely, dextrous piece on Monet (*PN Review* 274), which rhymes 'pleased' and 'elapsed', 'statement' and 'testament', 'aspired' and 'praised'. The judgement that McKendrick brings to bear in his rhymes is more Fullerian than Muldoonian, being attached to the meaning of the poem in a thoughtfully focused, rather than chancily associative, way:

> It's sunny up there on the moon tonight –
> deckchair weather, the better to survey
> the chapped rims of craters, the scurvy
>
> shapeless heaps of grey-brown dreck,
> the clean sweep of a miserly horizon.

Here the moon is resolutely, jocularly brought down to the level of that well-known site of imperfection, the Earth (elsewhere, in a poem addressed to Bernard O'Donoghue, McKendrick wryly remarks, 'Does earth take a capital letter? / you rightly wonder'). One is reminded, by way of contrast, of Auden's piece beginning 'This lunar beauty / Has no history'. Auden's lunar vista was mysteriously 'complete and early', untouched by the changes that harry our sub-lunar sphere, as the moon of the Aristotelian cosmology was. (And we may recall Auden's sardonic ribbing of aspirant space-travellers elsewhere: 'It's natural the Boys should whoop it up for / so huge a phallic triumph'. Auden was in some respects, as he once joked, with typical self-deprecation, 'a nineteenth-century man'.) By contrast, McKendrick's lunar scene fits with our reformed stargazing sensibility, alert to the new mundanity of the moon: nowadays, the moon is just another distant location that we might eventually inhabit. The pursuit of lunar settlement is now squarely in the realm of what Thomas Kuhn called 'normal science'. So artists should, if they are up to date with things, look elsewhere for wonder. The reader will be reminded of McKendrick's 'Out There' (the title poem of his 2012 collection), which ends, 'What once had been / where heaven was, is barren beyond imagining, / and never so keenly as from out there can / the lost feel earth's the only paradise'. Conflicted stuff! It feels spontaneous and oddly translucent, as if the poet were right there before us, stumbling towards the apt verbal formulation (as we see in some of Yeats's finer lines – e.g. 'That is not natural in an age like this', in 'No Second Troy'). It is far from endorsing anything obvious, far from reducing the complications that we should, when being honest about the shifted frontiers of our knowledge, confront.

McKendrick finds the new and old frontiers of wonder, some of which are still up there in the moon-direction, but way beyond the moon. Through an anecdote about a visit to a friend's grave, the final poem in the collection ('L'amor che move il sole e l'altre stelle') nudges us to consider the starry heavens above and the moral law within (those two inexhaustible sources of wonder that impressed Kant). And so we get, perhaps to our surprise, because McKendrick has been so diffident and unhectoring about it, a sort of model for conduct here, one based on decency and duty. In *Drypoint*, McKendrick triumphs again: with tact and humour, he reminds us of our terrestrial responsibilities while turning our minds to those things that can inspire us. When we are properly attentive to such work, 'No burnisher exists / to smooth that out or to restore / the calm clear surface of [our] thoughtlessness'.

Some Contributors

Francesca Brooks is Lecturer in Old English at University College Cork. A writer of poetry and essays, she is also author of *Poet of the Medieval Modern: Reading the Early Medieval Library with David Jones*. **Fred Warren** is a writer and filmmaker based in West Dorset and co-founder of the arts collective Chasing Cow Productions. In 2023 he co-produced a radio dramatisation of Nikolai Zabolotsky's *The Triumph of Agriculture*. **Horatio Morpurgo** lives in the southwest of England, where he grew up. He helped to campaign for the first Marine Protected Area of significant size in English waters, in Lyme Bay. He writes on the environment and on European affairs for various magazines. **James Dowthwaite's** poems on Babylonian themes have appeared, amongst other places, in *The Dawntreader, The Fortnightly Review*, *The High Window*, *The Martello Journal* and *Strix*. He is based in Germany. **Joe Winter** taught English in London secondary schools. Details of his many books of poetry, translation, literary criticism and other matters can be found at joewinter-poet.com. **Fawzia Muradali Kane** is a Trinbagonian architect and poet, currently based in London. Her latest poetry collection is titled *Guaracara* (Carcanet 2025). **Sunil Iyengar** is editor of *The Colosseum Book of Contemporary Narrative Verse* (Franciscan University Press) and the author of a chapbook of poems, *A Call from the Shallows* (Finishing Line Press).

WWWW.PNREVIEW.CO.UK

Editors
Michael Schmidt
John McAuliffe

Editorial Manager
Andrew Latimer

Contributing Editors
Anthony Vahni Capildeo
Sasha Dugdale
Will Harris

Copyeditor
Maren Meinhardt

Designed by
Andrew Latimer

Editorial address
The Editors at the address on the right. Manuscripts cannot be returned unless accomp anied by a stamped addressed envelope or international reply coupon.

Trade distributors
Combined Book Services Ltd

Represented by
Compass IPS Ltd

ISBN 978-1-80017-475-7
ISBN 0144-7076

Subscriptions—6 issues
INDIVIDUAL–print and digital: £45; abroad £65
INSTITUTIONS–print only: £140; abroad £162
INSTITUTIONS–digital only: from Exact Editions (https://shop.exacteditions.com/gb/pn-review) to: PN Review, Main Library, University of Manchester, Oxford Road, Manchester, M13 9PP, UK

Subscriptions & Enquiries:
support@pnreview.co.uk

Supported by
Supported using public funding by ARTS COUNCIL ENGLAND